FIFTY-SIX MORE DEVOTIONS ON SHORT NOTICE

James Wilson

ABINGDON PRESS

Nashville

FIFTY-SIX MORE DEVOTIONS ON SHORT NOTICE

Copyright © 1994 by Abingdon Press

This book is printed on acid-free, recycled paper.

ISBN 0-687-12990-7

Scripture quotations are from the Revised Standard Version of the Bible, copyright 1946, 1952, 1971 by the Division of Christian Education of the National Council of the Churches of Christ in the USA. Used by permission.

94 95 96 97 98 99 00 01 02 03 — 10 9 8 7 6 5 4 3 2 1

MANUFACTURED IN THE UNITED STATES OF AMERICA

It goes without saying this work originated from the author's perspective as a dedicated effort to serve the risen Christ. No such work is an individual effort, however, and there are several whom I would like to acknowledge for their significant contributions.

First, my wife, Jackie, and my stepson, Brandon. Without their patience, love, advice, and support, there simply would not have been a book. I love them both very much.

Second, I would like to thank two very wonderful friends, Bill and Mildred, who have been a genuine source of inspiration in their Christian walk.

And finally, a lady named Peggy, without whose guidance and editorial efforts I would have been lost.

Contents

Let Your Light Shine

Call

Let all who would give God the glory for the blessing of life itself, gather that we might sing and lift our praise.

Prayer

Dear God, as we come together today, fill our lamps with your holy presence. Trim and shape us, Lord, that we may shine in the way you intended for us to bring light into the world. Through Christ our Lord we pray. Amen.

Scripture

Matthew 5:14-17

Hymns

"This Little Light of Mine"
"Forth in Thy Name"

The human ego is a most remarkable part of our created nature. So often our behavior is inversely related to the strength of our ego. For example, the loud and boisterous person who tends to try to overwhelm others with an air of importance and insensitivity almost certainly lacks the ego strength to feel secure about himself. And conversely, the person who tends to display a quiet strength and who can be comfortably involved in a conversation without having to dominate it probably has a very healthy ego strength. An ancient Chinese proverb says, "Strength never has to prove itself; it is."

In our passage today, Jesus is calling for us to allow the light of our Christian witness to shine openly for all the world to see. Obviously, lamps are not lit to perpetuate the darkness, but there is a part of our culture that suggests there is no modesty or humility in touting one's own accomplishments or greatness. In fact, to tout one's own better qualities would suggest, as was pointed out earlier, a lack of ego strength. Surely Jesus understood this.

In fact, to many people there is something quite offensive in Christians strutting around pompously proclaiming the perfection they received by virtue of their adoption into the family of God as brothers and sisters of Christ. It is offensive not because of any theological error concerning their adoption, but because they seem to be ignoring the very model of humility and modesty that Jesus himself, born King of Kings, chose to demonstrate. Many Christians are timid about letting their light shine for fear of being misunderstood.

But Jesus is very insistent that we as Christians should be letting our lights shine and demonstrating for all the world that the gospel of Christ is real. Letting our light shine is not an optional assignment intended for any Christians who may feel a need to earn a little extra credit with God. Letting our light shine is a primary function of the church and all who would be called Christians.

There are a few facets of "light shining" and doing good works we as Christians need to keep in mind. The central feature in allowing one's light to shine is to share the gospel or good news. What exactly is this good news we have to share with the world? Through Christ, God offers us mercy and grace and when we accept Christ as our personal Lord and Savior, we are forgiven and become children of God. At this point, some are probably thinking "shining" is sounding a great deal like "strutting," to which Christians would answer, "Not at all!"

Letting our light shine is not strutting. Let us consider two occasions in the scriptures when two special people are letting their light shine. First, let us consider the Samaritan woman at the well with whom Jesus spoke concerning her sinful relationships with men. After being forgiven by the Lord, the woman ran back into her community and told everyone she could find about Jesus. Imagine for a moment you live in her community and she came running up to you with her story. Is it likely she would be telling you, "Hey, I met this man at the well and he told me I was finally good enough to be in God's kingdom!" Not likely! You know her and the sort of life she has been leading. Instead, she probably would have come up to you and excitedly told you, "I met this wonderful man at the well named Jesus and he knew what a terrible mess I've made of my life. He knew all about me and he told me I was forgiven. Me, the one who has never managed to get life right, God can forgive even me. You've got to meet this Jesus. He is saying God loves and will forgive even people like me!" The woman was letting her light shine, and she had good news for a hurting world.

Let us consider the apostle Paul. Have you ever read in the Scriptures where Paul wrote of how after his years of training as a pharisee and his outstanding service around the temple he had finally been considered worthy to be included in the kingdom of God? No, because Paul never wrote any such thought! But we do read Paul's testimony of how even he, the chief of sinners, was forgiven and was welcomed into the kingdom of God. Some would suggest Paul was only being modest and possibly even exaggerating a bit when he referred to himself as the chief among sinners. Really? Paul, you must remember, when Christ called him on the road to Damascus, was carrying the authorizing paperwork to arrest and eliminate Christians in an attempt to stop the spread of this new sect Paul hated so bitterly. Paul was part of the opposition to God and Christ. The good news Paul shared for all to hear was that even he, unworthy and once a devout and outspoken enemy to Christ, had been forgiven and made welcome in the kingdom of God, so there is room for you.

For those who feel, "But I'm not worthy to spread the gospel," you are exactly right and as we have seen you are in very good company! The good news we have to share is even unworthy people like us who repent and turn to the Lord will be forgiven and joyously welcomed into the kingdom of God. The truth is nobody is actually worthy before God; there are just some who have not yet faced up to this truth.

So when we let our light shine, we are not saying how good and worthy we ourselves are; instead we are sharing with others how, through Christ, God has made it possible for even sinners like us to be forgiven. Everyone who comes to Christ will be welcome. No strutting or ego boasting in this message, is there?

Jesus also commands Christians to live in such a way that others will see our good works. "See" is an important word. If we are truly letting our light shine, we are not telling everyone how good we are or Jesus would have called us to let people "hear" about our good works. We are to be doing the little things that show people we genuinely care. We are to do these things because they are the right things to do, not because we want recognition.

The young manager of a quick service restaurant watched as a bus load of touring senior church people stopped for lunch. Hundreds of miles away from home, the tour was now less than fifty miles from its destination. One couple on the bus had been experiencing some motion sickness and were simply not feeling comfortable with returning to the bus for the last leg of the trip. The manager, noticing how uncomfortable the couple was, offered to take the couple to their motel in his personal vehicle when he got off work in about an hour. Remarkably, the bus load of church people were overwhelmed by the young manager's kindness and consideration, but wasn't his offer to help exactly the sort of good work Jesus had called for his followers to be doing in the world?

In today's passage, Jesus commends us to let our lights shine and to be about good works for all the world to see. If we share the gospel with the world, we will not be boasting and we will not be strutting, and we might even be surprised about the ways the Lord will be able to use our witness.

Prayer

Dear Lord, give us the courage to witness and the sensitivity to see the needs of those around us that we might truly let our light shine. Through Christ we pray. Amen.

An Irony

Call

Blessed are the meek and humble, says the Lord! Let us all be humble in spirit as we enter the house of the Lord.

Prayer

O God, touch our hearts this morning with your sensitivity to those whose hearts are burdened and whose needs are great. Some who are in need will not even lift their voices to cry for help, but with your loving vision, we will see and hear them. Through Christ our Lord we pray. Amen.

Scripture

Luke 4:16-30 (possibly best read at the end of the message)

Hymns

"Come, Sinners, to the Gospel Feast"
"Take My Life, and Let It Be"

The church calendar for the week seems to be almost overlapping with committee meetings, activities, and programs. Not that this is so extraordinary—activity is usually seen as the sign of a healthy church and First Church has been a very active church for as long as anyone can remember.

Monday is normally the pastor's day off, but this Monday morning a special committee will be having an important meeting with some computer specialists about how best to upgrade the church computer. The present computer, now almost three years old, is not capable of running some of the newer and more powerful programs the office staff wants to add into the system.

Hardly a moment of the day Monday is to be wasted. During a working lunch for the senior adult group in the fellowship hall, plans for their two-week-long bus tour next summer will be finalized. Only thirty five are now signed up to go, and some adjustments in the bonus packages to their tour may have to be made.

Monday afternoon will be set aside for an important meeting with the architect concerning the remodeling of the sanctuary and office areas of the church physical plant. This meeting is intended to answer any last-minute questions before taking the final recommendations to the full building committee later that evening. The early remodeling plans and cost figures were so extensive that many members on the building committee were already considering the possibility of simply selling the current property and relocating. These two meetings will decide which course of action would be the wisest to bring for

consideration before the whole congregation.

The daytime schedule for Tuesday is largely filled with women's activities. From nine to ten o'clock will be a craft workshop and from ten to eleven an exercise class. From eleven until noon the entire women's group will hold its main monthly meeting, with a guest speaker on nutrition and weight control. Lunch for the ladies is being billed as "Dining in Fashion," a combination light lunch and fashion show sponsored by the women's wear stores in the mall. Then, following lunch, will come the meetings of the various women's committees and subcommittees planning future programs, Bible studies, activities, and fund raising events.

Tuesday evening will largely be consumed by two important meetings. The finance committee will meet at six o'clock, followed by the full church board meeting at eight. Budgets and future plans, especially the remodeling project, will all receive serious consideration, even if final decisions are not to be made Tuesday evening. This board meeting could last for some time.

Wednesday looks like a light day on the calendar; however, there are some regular weekly meetings no one ever bothers to write down any more. Much of the morning will be spent in the weekly church staff meeting. Wednesday afternoon will be set aside for education and youth planning and for preparations for the midweek service.

Thursday morning will be filled with a variety of groups meeting. The crafts group will meet again, and a number of the women's Bible study groups will be meeting. Thursday morning is also the regular time for the prayer group to meet and lift whatever personal or church concerns they have to the Lord in prayer. For the office staff, Thursday is the day the weekly newsletter will go out, and this particular Thursday is also the day quarterly giving statements are to be mailed.

Thursday afternoon is very much focused on the music program of the church. The several choirs in all age ranges, handbell choirs, and musicians will meet throughout the afternoon and on into the early evening hours. Apart from the Saturday morning second rehearsal for the chancel choir, these will be the only times the choirs will go through their music for this week until just before the service on Sunday morning.

Thursday evening, several more church committees will meet, including the evangelism and personnel committees and a special committee arranging a new church color photo directory to be printed. This particular Thursday evening, the junior high department has planned a trip for the young people in one of the church vans to the junior high away game.

Friday will see the senior adults back in force with several senior adult activities scheduled throughout the morning and a lunch set for noon. Friday afternoon will seem fairly quiet as most of the final preparations are being completed for the Sunday services and education programs.

Of course Saturday will be full of youth activities and this week there will also be two church committee meetings. Sunday will then follow with its worship services and education programs. And finally, of course, will come Monday and the cycle will begin all over again.

Throughout the week, the senior pastor has studied and labored over a scripture passage the Lord seems to have led the pastor to use for this Sunday's message. (Read all of Luke 4:16-30 or at least verses 18 and 19 here.)

For whatever reason, this has been one of those hectic weeks and nothing seems to be falling into place as far as a message from this passage. The pastor is quite certain the Lord has something special to be delivered this Sunday from this passage, but as the hours are growing agonizingly short, nothing is clear yet.

And the Lord said . . . (reread verses 18 and 19).

Prayer

Dear Lord, give us the wisdom to hear your words and understand the love we are to be sharing with the world around us. Help us to see beyond our own needs and comfort to see a hurting and wounded world needing so desperately to receive your healing and love. Through Christ our Lord we pray. Amen.

In Spirit

Call

Let all who would worship the Lord God Almighty, in spirit and in truth, gather this day to lift our voices in praise and in song.

Prayer

O Lord, draw our hearts ever closer to truly understanding that your kingdom is not of this world. Help us to more fully comprehend how to live and to worship in the spirit. In Christ we pray. Amen.

Scripture

John 4:19-26

Hymns

"Spirit of the Living God"
"There Is a Balm in Gilead"

These past several hundred years since the time of Martin Luther and the beginning of the Reformation have certainly not been the only period in Judeo-Christian history marked by divisions and denominationalism. Even in Jesus' day there was an irreconcilable division between those in Samaria who worshiped on Mt. Gerizim and those who worshiped at the Temple in Jerusalem.

Both Samaria and Judah were once a part of the powerful kingdom built and ruled first by David and finally by Solomon. After Solomon's death, however, came the division of the kingdom into two countries—the northern called Israel and the southern called Judah. Of course with Jerusalem and the original Temple being situated in Judah, and with Judah essentially considering itself to be a theocracy, it seems inevitable Israel, which later became known as Samaria, would eventually, for political reasons, have needed to establish its own temple.

Following the period of the Babylonian captivity, the split between Judah and Samaria had taken on a strongly religious tone clearly symbolized by the two temple locations, and neither had any intention of making any concessions for the sake of unity. So, as the Samaritan woman asked Jesus which of the two temple locations was the true place of worship, she may well have been voicing a question many people of her day who simply wished to sincerely worship God were probably at least thinking.

Let us try for a moment, to hear the extraordinary answer Jesus gave as the Samaritan woman might have heard it some two thousand years ago. The question as she presented it was simply a multiple choice question. "Which of the two temples is the true temple? A. Mt. Gerizim or B. Jerusalem." No other alternatives were open for consideration.

Although many historians credit the Hebrew people for having first introduced the understanding of God as being both universal—that is not regional or territorial—and transcendent, or God as being the creator of all nature and not dependent upon nature and the nature cycles, believers in the woman's time were still taught the proper and best approach to worship was through the sacrificial system and supporting the temple. Thus Jesus' answer of how true worship of God would no longer depend upon the temple at either Mt. Gerizim or Jerusalem was a totally revolutionary concept. Jesus was telling the Samaritan woman it was neither "A" nor "B" but another answer altogether; beyond the physical limitations of temples or sanctuaries, and in the spiritual heart.

Christians have probably been taught the concept of worshiping God in the spirit for so many generations that we have taken this incredible blessing for granted. But it is in this spiritual understanding of worship we find the confidence to know that as we walk in the woods and are wonder-struck by the creation around us, God hears our praise. As we are in the strains and stresses of the worst situations in life and lift our voices from the depths of our soul to God, we can know we are heard. As we sit in the waiting rooms of hospitals in even the most remote regions of the world and whisper a prayer for a loved one in surgery, we know God is with us. Spiritual worship has given us a freedom to lift our prayers before the Lord at any time and from within absolutely any circumstances and know we are heard.

But there is a greater meaning beyond just freedom of access in prayer before the Lord to worship. Implicit also in this concept of worshiping God in the spirit is how the basic essence of our life now becomes a symbol of worship. Rather than a sacrificial system demonstrating our penitent nature, the very way we live becomes the mode for worship and giving praise to God. Over and over we read in the stories and parables in the Gospels of how the way to express gratitude for having received God's blessings or forgiveness is by giving to those who are in need and forgiving others as we have been forgiven. For example, in Matthew 18, the king was angered by the slave who had been forgiven his massive debt of ten thousand talents, only to try to imprison another slave who owed the first slave just a very small amount. Worshiping in spirit involves our whole attitude toward life and those around us.

Even our everyday language still reflects an understanding of how our attitude conveys our witness. Phrases commonly used today such as describing a person as being "mean spirited" or how a person has "a gentle spirit" or "a loving spirit" still demonstrate our understanding of the relationship between our way of life and the condition of our spirit or soul.

Jesus brought us a gift that opened the door for us to finally move away from the mechanical forms of worship. What did it matter if sinners brought the most perfect and beautiful sacrifice to the Temple at Jerusalem if the sinners' hearts were not truly repenting of their sins? On the other hand, Jesus was now saying if sinners are truly repenting of their sins, God certainly needs no sacrifice in order to forgive them. And if we truly repent of our sins, we will endeavor to do our very best not to repeat those sins. Not because we cannot be forgiven again, but because we have seen these actions are not the way we want to live. Our lives begin to reflect our spirits, and thus become a profound method of worship before the whole world in which we live.

Today there may be divisions and denominations in the body of Christ we call the Church, but still the true worship remains in the spirit. No wonder the Samaritan woman at the well was excited at the news she had received from Jesus. The Lord God Almighty, creator of all of the universe, loves each and every sinner so much that the door has been opened to come before God's holy throne with only a whisper from a sinner's heart. Let us hear then the words of Christ and truly worship and give God praise!

Prayer

Dear God, thank you for opening the door for our forgiveness and salvation even when we were so lost we did not know the depth of our sins. Thank you for loving your children so much you would hear every word we would share with you. We lift our hearts in praise, dear Lord. In Christ we pray. Amen.

Send Me

Call

Come, let us gather in the house of the Lord all who would hear and carry the message of Christ to all the nations!

Prayer

O God, you called and sent the prophets to carry your word to the children of Israel; and you have commissioned your church to carry your word into the world today. Speak to us again, Lord, and call us each one to the tasks you would have us be about in your kingdom that those of every nation might hear the good news of Christ. In your holy name we pray. Amen.

Scripture

Isaiah 6:1-8

Hymns

"Here I Am, Lord"
"For the Fruits of This Creation"

How many of us have ever read this familiar passage describing Isaiah's acceptance of God's call to be a prophet and felt a noble urge to stand tall before the Lord and declare, "Send Me!" There often seems to be something alluring and almost mystical about the blessing of God's special call on a person's life, and who would not want history to recall us as having been among the great saints of the faith?

But have you ever wondered as well about the paradox of God's blessing? Has it ever really caught your attention what has happened to these specially blessed called people of the Lord?

For example, who could imagine a greater blessing than was Mary's to have been chosen to be the mother of the Christ? But how many of us even today, when the social pressures are much less than they were in that day, could have handled the stress of the virgin birth? Or who among us would have sought a blessing that would have us fleeing for our life before even a year had passed? Or how many of us could have withstood the agony of watching the political intrigue developing and finally the crucifixion of our child? But, you say, surely Mary was an exceptional case of God's blessing. Possibly, but let's quickly glance at a few others.

How about John the Baptist? By Jesus' own account, John was the greatest born under the old covenant. John, chosen to proclaim the coming of Christ, was a man of truth and honor. But would you like to dress in animal skins and live on a diet of locusts and wild honey? Oh, but that was then, you say. Even then, John's life-style was strange and think how uncomfortable most of us are today if we are the least bit different or out of step with what everyone else is wearing or eating.

And how did John the Baptist fare? We all know the story of what happened when John, the man called of God, could not turn his back on Herod's immoral involvement with Philip's wife Herodias. Herod eventually had John beheaded. Are God's moral standards that important to us?

Or how many of us would like to have the special blessing the Apostle Paul received from the Lord? Paul, as we all know, was a great scholar and missionary. But how many of us believe so devoutly in sharing the good news of Christ we would be willing to face crowds of people intent on stopping or even killing us? How many of us believe so deeply in carrying the message of Christ throughout the world we would risk our life over and over again in dangerous means of travel or precarious circumstances just to deliver the gospel? And how many of us love the Lord so much we would gladly sit in a Roman jail and eventually die before we would deny our allegiance to Christ? God's blessing can come with a price.

And what about Stephen, the first martyr of the early church? Would we seek God's blessing knowing it came with the risk that one day we might have to stand firm on the truth amid a world that not only does not want to hear the truth but is so intent on silencing us it finally resorts to stoning us to death? God's blessing can mean we may have some pretty serious choices to make.

Throughout the scriptures and the history of the church, the paradox of God's blessing often coming with a price has been seen over and over again. From Abraham and Sarah, called to lay their blessed son Isaac before the Lord, through the prophets who died at the rejecting hands of the very people God had sent them to save, and on into the early church period when Christians who refused to bow to the Roman demands of allegiance faced hungry lions, the cost of truly receiving the blessings of God have been real.

But you ask, surely these are the extremes of the past? People are seldom called upon to risk their lives these days, are they? Our answer of course depends on what we mean by life. If we mean do people still physically risk their lives going into unsafe areas to share the message of Christ, of course, they do. Missionaries in some foreign environments are still at risk as are more and more Christian missionaries who go into our own inner city gang-controlled communities. Yes, believers are still willing to place their lives in the balance that others might hear the good news of God's redeeming love.

But there is a more subtle meaning to life that may bring this question closer to home for all of us. If we are asking whether the followers of Christ are still called upon to risk the comfortable lifestyle to which they may have become accustomed in order to stand firm for the gospel of Christ, then the answer may well be many more Christians are called to do this than we might think. Standing firm for what is morally just and right may indeed come with a price. Would we be willing to risk losing what luxuries in life we may have rather than compromise and give in to the argument "but everybody is doing it that way." "Are we willing to risk our life-style?" is a much harder question.

Is Christ so important to us we would risk the disfavor and even the rejection of our friends and neighbors? Who among us in our heart has not asked the Lord, "But Jesus, you don't really expect me to risk all of that, do you?" And our risen Lord loves us still.

When the Lord asked, "Whom shall I send?"—Isaiah answered, "Here am I Lord. Send me." We can dream and we can have noble thoughts, but until we truly are willing to place all we have before

Christ, including our life-style, we're probably not as serious as we need to be in seeking the call and blessings of God.

People, the Lord still calls to us, and the Lord still blesses those who will respond. The Lord is calling right now. "Whom shall I send?" If deep down in your heart as you hear this, you are saying, "I'd go but don't ask me to give up my car or the TV or my clothes" or whatever it is that is important to you, well, I have good news. It is you God is talking to today. Will you finally set the standards of the world aside and accept the incredible blessings God desires to give you by standing tall and answering, "Here am I Lord. Send me."

Prayer

Dear Lord, so often we have avoided your call because we were comfortable and we were afraid to risk what we could see for the eternity we cannot see. Bless us, O God, and send us from this place into the world as your messengers of the good news. Through Christ our Lord we pray. Amen.

I'd Rather Die for You, Lord

Call

Come! Let all who would seek to live their lives in the service of Christ, our living Lord, gather this day and worship.

Prayer

Dear Lord, as we gather today, we ask that you touch our hearts and give us the strength and the courage to daily

live so that others might know our commitment to you is genuine. Through Christ we pray. Amen.

Scripture

Philippians 1:19-30

Hymns

"Are Ye Able"
"Go Forth for God"

There are few experiences that bring a deeper sense of warmth and satisfaction to our lives than having the privilege of watching other Christians experience growth in their spiritual lives. Sometimes spiritual periods of significant growth come quickly; sometimes they come gradually over a period of years. Almost always, however, spiritual growth requires time in studying the Scriptures and serious personal prayer.

At a recent pastors' meeting the group heard an inspiring example of one group's spiritual growth. It started late the previous summer when several church members asked their pastor if it would be possible to have a pastor-led study and prayer group for those who felt a need to spend a little more time in Bible study and prayer. The pastor agreed, and the group began to meet in the fall just as the trees were beginning to change colors. Six people attended the first hour-long meeting. They spent about forty-five minutes in Bible study and discussion and the remaining fifteen minutes in prayer.

The topic for that first meeting was Jesus' command for each who would be known as a Christian to be ready to accept the cross the Lord would give them. The image of the cross raised the question of whether or not those present at the study were truly prepared in their hearts to commit all they had, even their lives if necessary, to standing for the Lord. As long as the discussion remained on a philosophical level, there was little hesitation in everyone stating their willingness to die for Christ. The discussion made it fairly clear, however, that the participants were aware that very few people are actually called upon to die for Christ today in this

country. The odds seemed to make such a commitment a pretty safe bet actually. The first meeting closed with everyone agreeing to do two things. First, each one would look up a case where a missionary in this century had been martyred and be prepared to share what he or she had found the next week. Second, each person agreed to think and pray about whether he or she was really willing and ready to die for the Lord.

As the meeting opened the second week, it was readily apparent they had done their assignments. One person shared a personal moment from his prayer time when he had said to God, "Lord, I'd be willing to die for you, but do I have to go through all this pain?" And the shared stories of the martyred Christian missionaries were replete with descriptions of pain and suffering. Somehow, in hearing the stories of those who had in reality taken up the cross and died in the Savior's service, there came a different understanding of the seriousness of the commitment we each make when we become Christians. If being a Christian means having a willingness to follow the Lord and go where the Lord sees fit to carry the gospel into the world, even into places where missionaries have already been killed, then perhaps we aren't so willing to agree to that sort of commitment. After all, each of those present had a family and each of them had jobs and responsibilities. This new dimension to being willing to die for the Lord would require much more study and prayer.

Thanksgiving week granted an additional week's reprieve or agony, depending on how each group member experienced facing the challenge. When the third meeting of the study group came, the handiwork of the Holy Spirit was clearly apparent among the group members. The number in attendance had suddenly doubled. The spouses, having already endured hours of soul searching discussion with their mates, decided they might as well be involved first-hand.

During this meeting, each of the original six people shared his or her path to arriving at a new level of personal commitment and a now genuine commitment to following Christ, whatever the consequences, even if it meant dying in his service. There was a soberness and a gravity about the third meeting, with each couple obviously in harmony and totally dedicated to their decision. The meeting was also marked with an underlying sense of joy and well being, the sort of feeling that comes when you know you have just done something very important and that you have done it well. Like the previous two, the third meeting was also marked with moments of levity as that generated by the comment, "I'm still not thrilled about the pain part, Lord." It would be fair to say there was a glow present in the pastor's study that evening.

It would not be until January that the group again returned to the subject of personal commitment. Late in the month the group, now too large to meet in the pastor's study, would hear the apostle Paul speak in Philippians of "living for Christ." Now the unsettled atmosphere once present as the group struggled with being willing to die for the Lord returned. The commitment to "live for Christ," as obvious as the idea is, was a much different question than being willing to die for the Lord, and strangely enough, the gravity of the

commitment to live for Christ had never really struck them before. Living for Christ was fraught with all sorts of frightening dimensions. What if their friends and neighbors thought they were "weird" or that they had suddenly "got religion." One group member said, "The Lord never seems to leave well enough alone. I was just getting used to being willing to die for the Lord and now God has changed the question."

The following week's meeting was filled with an atmosphere of celebration. Not everyone had moved to a conclusion on the question of being willing to live for Christ as quickly as the original couples, but with tears of joy those six couples shared how, as the week progressed, they could not help feeling that if they were going to trust the Lord they had to trust all the way. At this point, the person most likely to come up with a poignant comment added one that pretty much summarized what several in the group had experienced at some point in the week. This person explained how, about midweek, after some intense soul searching and prayer, that thought had crossed his mind, "I think I'd rather die for you, Lord!"

One can only wonder if the apostle Paul had experienced something like this group's spiritual pilgrimage that led him to write the scripture passage expressing his willingness to either live or die for the Christ he loved so much. The scriptures, if we will only hear them, share with us a living eternal faith available to each and every person who will seek it today. But spiritual growth and soul searching are always difficult. Are you ready to state before God that you are truly willing to die for and to live for the Lord?

Dear Lord, we thank you for the loving patience you lead us with to grow spiritually. Sometimes, in our pride, we feel we have a much deeper faith than we actually have once we ask ourselves if we are willing to serve you whatever the consequences. Lord, hear our hearts' desire to be your children and help lead us to mature in our faith. Through Christ our Lord we pray. Amen.

Who Do You Say That I Am?

Call

Come, let us lift our voices together in song and praise to proclaim Jesus Christ is Lord.

Prayer

Dear Lord, help us to search our souls that we might answer for you today the same questions you once asked the disciples and which you have asked of Christians through the ages. Amen.

Scripture

Matthew 16:13-17

Hymns

"Where He Leads Me"
"I Stand Amazed in the Presence"

In this passage from Matthew, we are given a glimpse into one of the private times Jesus spent with the disciples away from public view. These must have been wonderful times for the disciples—times when they were given both special attention and the opportunity to receive spiritual insights uniquely preparing them for their roles in the ministry of the early church. These less public times, like this occasion when Jesus renames Simon the fisherman Peter, the man of faith, must have been precious memories for the disciples throughout the rest of their ministries.

But these private times were important for Jesus as well—moments where he not only had an opportunity to teach and share the true nature of God's kingdom with the disciples, but times when he could be personal and relax within an atmosphere of friendship.

These private moments with his disciples also, as we see occurring in today's passage, allowed Jesus an opportunity for evaluation. When Jesus asked the disciples who people were saying he really was, the answer Jesus received gave him some measure of how well the crowds were receiving and comprehending his teachings about the kingdom of God. The answer made it obvious that most of the hearers had yet to comprehend the fact that Jesus is God's promised Messiah.

Jesus then seeks to probe how well the disciples themselves are growing spiritually by changing the question and asking who they think he is. Simon, who never seems to be hesitant at saying pretty much what he is thinking, calls

Jesus the Christ, the son of the living God, a profession of faith so profound it still remains at the center of the Christian walk today.

But let's imagine for a moment that this passage is the focus of your next Sunday school lesson. This is not the first time you have studied this passage and as the time for class draws near, you dread the discussion you know is coming. It is almost inevitable some argument will develop over the relationship between the Greek meaning of Peter as "a small stone" or possibly today's nickname, "Rocky," and the word Jesus used for rock in the phrase "upon this rock" as in "a large rock." It hardly seems possible, as many times as Jesus took the time to explain to the disciples exactly what certain teachings meant, that he did not expand on this teaching. Surely he knew the many differences among Christians this passage would generate.

Time has come to start class, and the regular teacher still has not entered the room. At the last minute in walks a smiling fellow who explains he will be filling in as the teacher today and the class can just call him Pete. The class opens with a prayer, followed by the reading of the scripture passage. Several ask questions seeking to get to know Pete better, but he is obviously a gifted teacher and the focus remains on the lesson.

Just as surely as sunrise the topic turns to the meaning of the phrase "upon this rock," and it is easy to tell the sides are preparing to line up and do battle. But this time will be different as Pete intervenes with a challenging question: "Although some across the centuries have tended to feel 'upon this rock' is the critical portion of this passage, I've always believed the question, 'But who do you say that I am?' was the heart of the issue. So let's take a moment now, just as if Jesus were sitting here talking to us personally, and what would you say if he asked you, 'But who do you say that I am?' "

It could not have taken more than a minute or so to go around the room with everyone giving what they felt was the required answer, "Jesus is the Christ, son of the living God."

As the last person answers, like a group of dutiful children finishing our chores, we seek to get back to our play in debating "upon this rock." But Pete will have none of this and rephrases the question. "I'm glad," Pete says, "each of you knows who Jesus is, but exactly how do you say Jesus is the Christ, the son of the living God?"

Total silence hangs over the room. It is as if a thick cloud layer has moved in, preventing even a single beam of light from shining through. Puzzled and blank looks are everywhere as no one dares to say the obvious, "We just say it." Pete is obviously asking for something more than "with our words." One timid soul finally speaks up and answers in a tone sounding a good deal more like a question, "With our lives?"

Pete smiles approvingly and again rephrases the question into, "And how do you say Jesus is the Christ with your life?"

If by some magic we could hear the thoughts of the group as they struggle with Pete's last question, we would probably be amazed. One person is thinking, "Who is this guy, anyway, and why all these hard questions?" Another wonders, "What am I supposed to say that won't make me look as stupid as I'm feeling?" Still another thinks, "What situation could I describe to help demonstrate what I believe is the Christian life?"

It is easy for us to observe this class setting complete with a visit from a stranger intended to remind us of the apostle Peter, while in the safety of our imaginations. But, no matter how imaginary the characters and the setting, the questions posed to the class are the same questions the followers of Christ have had to answer since the very foundation of the church. First, "who do you say that Jesus is?" Of course we begin by giving our answer with our words as we confess Jesus is the Christ and our Lord. But our words alone are not enough, and we must then search out how we might best demonstrate Christ's Lordship in our life is real. Of course our actions truly do speak louder than our words, so the best way we can say who Christ really is to us is through the way we live our life. And how might we best live our life as a Christian witness? In the twenty-second chapter of Matthew, we hear Jesus give us only two commandments. The first is to love God with all our heart, our soul, and our mind. The second is to love our neighbor as we love ourself.

How many of us, if we were to be completely honest, would have been comfortable being in our imaginary class facing the questions Pete was asking? Specifically, how many of us realize these very questions Pete was asking are being asked of all Christians every day by those around us who observe our lives firsthand? Most important of all, however, how many of us remember the risen Christ, with us every second of every day, who also observes that all Christians live their answer to, "And who do you say that I am?"

Prayer

Dear Lord, so often we have divided our lives into times we would be holy and times we would be of the world. Forgive us, Lord, and give us the strength and courage to be full-time Christians—not just part-time followers. Amen.

Green Apple Theology

Call

Let all who struggle with the challenges of our modern age and seek to serve our living Lord know peace in our heart and join together this day to raise our voices as one in praise to our eternal God.

Prayer

Dear Lord, help us today to understand better your ways and your desires for our lives. Help us to see beyond the instant demands of our age to see your eternity. Help us to know and display for all to see a living faith based not on a belief in ourselves, but on our faith in your Lordship. Amen.

Scripture

I Corinthians 6:12-20

Hymns

"Ask Ye What Great Thing I Know"
"Freely, Freely"

The ambitious adult Sunday school class decided to start having a Bible study on Thursday evenings. The catalyst for this decision was the pastor's sermon the week before focused on encouraging people to spend a little more time reading the Bible. A weekly Bible study sounded exactly like what the pastor had hoped to accomplish.

After the decision to have the Thursday Bible study had been made and while everyone was feeling a sense of pride about their new commitment, a whole new series of questions suddenly appeared that obviously needed to be considered. They were the usual questions such as where would they meet, which part of the Bible would they study first, and possibly most important of all, did they want any sort of snacks or treats? In order, the answers were: they would rotate meeting in one another's homes; they would start with I Corinthians; and yes, they felt something light to eat would be nice.

The class selected I Corinthians because although everyone seemed to know about the thirteenth chapter, no one could really remember any other portion of this famous Pauline letter. And so it was decided, they would meet on Thursday evenings to hear again the words of Paul without the influence of any Bible commentaries or input from any sort of clergy.

For the first two weeks the Bible study met, everything was wonderful. The opening few chapters of Paul's first letter to the Corinthians seemed to speak volumes to these eager searchers about faith and the identity of a Christian. On the second week, chapter 4:3-4, in which Paul refuses to be about judging himself and where he explains the only true judgment is the judgment before the Lord, was a mild point of controversy, but the study concluded in harmony.

The third week, however, contained a very unsettling experience for the newly formed Bible study. It was during the third week that the participants reached the section beginning with chapter 6, verse 12. Did the apostle Paul actually mean to be saying "all things" were lawful for him now that he was a Christian? Surely "all things" was not what Paul was really trying to say. Suspecting there was something they were obviously missing about this passage, the study group decided maybe it was time to consult a commentary.

The commentary they selected added more food for thought than answers. The commentary not only confirmed Paul did indeed mean to say "all things" were legal for him, but it went on to discuss the concept of Christian freedom. Somehow the full impact of Christian freedom had never before really registered on the people who made up this Bible study group, and the freedom we receive as Christians remained the central topic of discussion for several weeks as the apostle Paul more fully developed his thoughts on true freedom in I Corinthians.

Perhaps there are others of us who, if given the opportunity, would join the Bible study group in their struggle to gain a fuller understanding of Paul's efforts to balance total personal freedom with ultimate personal responsibility for our behavior before the Lord. How could something be "lawful" or doable on the one hand and yet be harmful or bad on the other? All of this sounds strangely like doubletalk at points. Maybe a look at what an old hill preacher once called "Green Apple Theology" might help.

What an old preacher from the hills once suggested was that a lot of things in life are like green, unripe apples. As almost anyone who grew up with apple trees around can tell you, there are few

flavors in life that can top a fresh ripe apple picked directly from the tree. But most of those same folks, if they would admit it, would also tell you there are few lessons in life an impatient young person learns better than "the fate worse than death" that results from eating too many unripe green apples. And what makes it even worse is when your folks asked, as you lay there at death's door, wishing the end to this agony would come quickly, if you had eaten any of the green apples after they had warned you the apples weren't quite ready. Fortunately, one almost always recovers from the overconsumption of green apples, much the wiser person for having had the experience.

Many things in life are like those apples. Under the appropriate circumstances, like the ripe apples, they are wonderful. For example, pharmaceuticals used properly at the appropriate times can be wonderful. Pain medications and prescription drugs intended to help a person cope with stress and anxieties can literally be lifesaving when used properly. Those exact same medications when used improperly become like the abused green apples, but unfortunately not everyone recovers from drug overdosing. The pharmaceuticals are not inherently evil themselves, but the abusive use of them is certainly not a positive action on the part of the abuser.

Green Apple Theology may also help us understand how sex is not inherently good or bad. God created us as sexual beings and, in the proper context, the role God intended for sex is incredibly beautiful. However, sex can be just as tempting as those forbidden green apples. Paul is reminding us that as

Christians, we belong totally to the Lord. Our spirit, our mind, and our body belong to Christ and we have no business consuming sexual "green apples," a message many in today's world do not really want to hear.

Sometimes there can be helpful insights in the simplest of ideas. The old preacher's Green Apple Theology will most likely never find its way into the traditional theological studies as they are taught in Christian seminaries. Yet if this simple theology helps even a few believers understand the Christian freedom Paul writes about, it has served its purpose well.

Each of us must remember our salvation was purchased through the cross and is not earned through our faithful adherence to dietary laws or extensive legalistic social codes. Christian salvation is received through our living faith in the risen Christ. Let us then ask God to give us the wisdom to recognize the ripe apples in life intended for our enjoyment and that we be able to distinguish them from the green apples, so our witness might be true and faithful to Christ for all the world to see.

Prayer

Dear Lord, freedom and its corresponding responsibilities can be overwhelming. Guide us, Lord, that we might avoid the green apples in life and be the kind of loving accepting people you would have us to be. Through Christ our Lord we pray. Amen.

True or False

Call

Let all who are seeking to know God's leadership in their lives join together this day for worship.

Prayer

O God, you have told us that your ways are not our ways, but we need your personal guidance and leadership if we are to be able to see the difference between the two. Bless our hearts today with renewed insights to discern the ways of the world we have accepted. In Christ we pray. Amen.

Scripture

Romans 12:1-2

Hymns

"Take My Life, and Let It Be"
"Jesus Calls Us"

There are few things more unsettling than the unexpected. As human beings, we seem to take some degree of comfort in finding the world around us in the place and in the order we expect it to be.

Several years ago, a church located within sight of a major state university campus committed itself to starting an outreach program aimed at the on-campus students. The pastor and the youth director were both dynamic and most capable of working with college students. In only a few weeks college students began coming to the Sunday morning worship service. The first few were very traditionally dressed in suits or nice dresses. But a few weeks later, a few more students began to arrive for worship services and among these were some who were dressed in blue jeans, sport shirts, and sneakers. More than a few eyebrows were raised as some of the long-time church members began to question if reaching out to the college community had been such a good idea.

In another church, an evangelist showed up for one of the scheduled revival services during the week dressed in a set of navy blue hooded sweats. The distress among the congregation at seeing this obvious impropriety was more than a little apparent. Off to one side some of the church board members gathered and discussed whether or not someone should slip the evangelist aside and have a talk with him about this ungodly attire. It was agreed one of the board members should privately talk to the evangelist. Upon doing so the only response the board member received was a smile and a polite word of appreciation for his concern. The message that evening was about the role of John the Baptist, the unconventional prophet and cousin of Jesus. Somehow, at least a few in the congregation that evening probably had a better understanding of the discomfort John the Baptist may have generated through his choice of nontraditional attire.

And how about the role the automobile plays in many churches today? Is the pastor's car of an appropriate style, model, and price range to properly reflect the image of the church? For the congregation of very comfortable means, the pastor's automobile should at least be fairly new and nice. On the other hand, for the smaller and less affluent congregation, the pastor's vehicle probably should not be too expensive.

And what about the "look-see session" we tend to have gathered around the first appearance of new automobiles or trucks on the church parking lot? With the hood up and doors wide open, it appears the Sunday morning inspection could be as thorough as the final inspection at the factory where the vehicle was built.

And then there is our attraction within the church to that which is either new or old—new buildings, new programs, new parking areas, new choir robes, new sound systems, new hymnbooks, new carpeting in the sanctuary, new staff members, new musical instruments, new copy machines, new decorations for the holidays of the year, new almost everything, even an occasional new pastor.

Or we may have fixed our vision upon the old treasures in our church—the old building, the old sanctuary, the old piano, the old pulpit furniture, the old stained glass window, the old ways things were done, or the old almost anything to which one can attach a brass dedication plate and memories.

And of course very often a congregation will have some sort of feud going on like the one that began several years ago in a church board meeting. It has been so long now since that meeting few in the church can actually remember exactly what the hard feelings started over. The issue may have been over how best to use the money in the memorial fund or then again it may have been about one of the church personnel policies. It does not really seem to matter anymore. Today, the participants remember only how everyone on the other side of the issue, whatever it was, behaved and how unChristian those on the other side were. One does not quickly forget situations like those.

But few organizations in the community can boast of helping the truly needy of this world as does the church. God has been so generous in blessing so many church members with so much it only seems fitting to help the needy in some way. The hard part is usually in setting up a program that will help the truly needy but will not encourage people to be lazy. After all, the church resources designated for this sort of ministry are limited, and the help available needs to be used wisely or even these resources may disappear.

The computer and facsimile machine have totally revolutionized the way the church does business today almost as much as the affordable copy machine did a few years ago. There are computer programs available today for churches of almost every membership range that help make membership and offering recordkeeping a very manageable task. Some of the computer programs for churches will even do birthday mailings and other direct marketing features helpful in managing communications to both members and visitors. If one adds the abilities of the fax machine for

instantly transmitting and receiving reports and other documents to everything the computer will do, the church offices become almost as capable as many small-sized business offices today.

More and more accountability is becoming a popular theme in public education today as it has been in the business world for some time. In many areas students must first pass some sort of comprehensive test in order to graduate or pass out of the eighth grade level on into their high school work. Wouldn't it be interesting if someone would create some sort of test, maybe a true-false test, based on the scriptures to help us measure our spiritual growth personally and as congregations? Imagine opening the test booklet and there on the first page are the instructions and the first question:

Circle the answer of your choice for each of the following questions.

1. Christians are not conformed to this world.

True   False

Prayer

O God, sometimes we have let ourselves be so caught up in the ways and matters of this world we have lost track of what you created us to be. Teach us, Lord, to walk in your ways and to live by your standards. In Christ we pray. Amen.

Branches

Call

Come! Let all who seek to serve the Lord gather in his house and worship. Let our voices be lifted in praise and let our souls be filled with joy, for surely we have been blessed through God's infinite love and mercy.

Prayer

Dear Lord, as we gather together this day, renew our spirits that your love in us might shine brightly for all the world to see. We are your servants, Lord; renew our servant's heart. Through Christ we lift our prayer. Amen.

Scripture

John 15:4-5

Hymns

"I Need Thee Every Hour"
"O Young and Fearless Prophet"

We are the branches and Christ is the vine. Does this image of our relationship to Christ speak to your heart?

Do you know what "sweeps week" means in the world of television? "Sweeps week" comes every so often and it is when the overall network ratings, as well as individual programming ratings, are very closely checked. As a result each network and cable station tries to win the best rating it can by putting the most attractive programming they have to offer into the lineup. "Sweeps week" can sometimes mean better than normal programs are offered on television.

During a "sweeps week" a few years ago, Vince and Kathy, a young married student couple, had planned and looked forward to seeing a special Civil War program that was going to be aired on PBS. Both loved Civil War history, and they had worked extra hard getting their assignments done ahead of time so they would have this special evening to relax and enjoy the program totally guilt free.

Finally the big evening came, and just as Vince and Kathy were sitting down to watch their special program they heard a lot of commotion across the street. They looked out their front window and there was an emergency medical unit in front of the Taylors' house with many of the neighbors gathered around to see what was happening. Very quickly the EMTs came out with Mr. Taylor on a litter.

Kathy and Vince knew the Taylors and visited them as often as their busy schedule allowed. They knew the Taylors had no relatives living nearby and Mrs. Taylor did not drive. With a quick glance at each other, Kathy and Vince knew the TV special would have to wait and they lovingly took the shocked and scared Mrs. Taylor up to the hospital where they stayed with her until the wee hours of the morning.

Mr. Taylor was in the hospital for ten days, and sure enough Vince and Kathy rearranged their lives to see to it that Mrs. Taylor got to the hospital every morning and that she made it home safe and sound every night. Homecoming for Mr. Taylor was quite a celebration, and life in the neighborhood returned to normal. About a week later there was a little knock at Vince and Kathy's door just as the sun was setting. As Kathy opened the door, there stood Mrs. Taylor with a big smile and the most wonderful looking berry pie Kathy had ever seen. Mrs. Taylor had come to say thanks for the love these two special young people had shown her.

Are we beginning to see some fruit on Vince and Kathy's spiritual branches?

Christine was a department head for a major aerospace company and had worked there for almost fifteen years. One day her supervisor came to her and explained that John was going to be transferred to her department. This was to be John's last chance. He had made several serious mistakes in other departments already, and the supervisor clearly implied to Christine that John's production was low and he was simply not worth much more time in the company.

The very first day John came to Christine's department was a bad one. About midmorning as Christine came walking over to check on him John looked up, saw her coming and smiled just as he was about to drop some valuable parts into the wrong treatment process that would have ruined them. Christine, seeing what was about to happen, signaled for John to stop and the parts were saved. As she came closer, Christine could see a look in John's eyes that spoke volumes as he could not believe he was just about to make another terrible mistake.

Christine, like all good management people, cared about her people so she asked John to step into her office for a minute. Not once did she threaten John

and not once did she complain. They talked about his family and the activities John's children were involved in. Finally Christine explained to John how she had faith in him and that for the time being, he would have no job quotas and would have no pressure to increase his production. Instead she asked John to slow down and take his time so he could get things right.

About a year later John had not made a single mistake and was actually named the company's most improved employee. Christine had a big lump in her throat as she watched John receive his certificate. Are we beginning to see some fruit on Christine's spiritual branches?

So many times we tend to think if we are not parting the Red Sea like Moses did, or if we are not planting new churches throughout the world as Paul did, then we are not bearing fruit on our branches. And many of us figure if we are not in some form of full-time professional ministry we have no fruit we can bring before the Lord. Well, what about Vince and Kathy or Christine? The names have been changed here to protect people's privacy, but their stories are true. Deep down in your heart, don't you feel Christ smiled as these events unfolded and in the eyes of God there was fruit on their branches?

Everyday events are where we make everyday decisions whether we will serve the Lord or will seek other concerns. All three of the people we have seen today know and love and consciously seek to serve Christ. Christine once brought her broken life before the cross and through God's mercy was given a new life. Kathy and Vince were struggling every day to make ends meet and knew in their hearts the ends only came together because God was a part of their lives.

So where do we start? How do we begin to let our branches bring forth fruit? A good place to start might be to look at whatever in our life was broken that we laid before the cross—whatever area we had failed in and knew we were sinners before the Lord. Mercy and grace started for us with the cross and not with our own merit, and we have received both with all of God's love. As the mercy and grace of our Lord Jesus Christ abides in us, let us share it with all we meet, that our branches might bear an abundant harvest of fruit.

Prayer

O Lord, forgive us when we have taken your blessings for granted and failed to share them with all we meet. Touch our hearts today, Lord, that we might leave today committed to allowing your fruit to come forth in our lives. Through Christ our Lord we pray. Amen.

Super Shinin' Sheep

Call

Let us gather together this day, all who would know the living presence of Christ. Let us lift our voices in praise before the Lord!

Prayer

Dear Lord, draw us together today as one flock, fully aware that you are our good shepherd. Soften our hearts, Lord, with the sound of your voice, and lead us into the paths of life that will give living witness that you are God. Amen.

Scripture

Psalm 23 and John 10:27

Hymns

"Here I Am"
"I Am Thine, O Lord"

As a greater and greater percentage of the world population now lives in urban population areas, fewer and fewer of us are familiar with the everyday agrarian images so common within the scriptures. For that matter, only a very small percentage of the population on the North American continent ever had a close association with the raising of sheep. Yet both of our scripture passages for today draw precisely upon these shepherding images to convey their deepest meanings, images the pastoral culture of biblical times would have readily recognized and understood. Most of us today, however, must struggle to discover the richness of meaning contained within the shepherding images Jesus used and that are at the heart of what is probably the best known of all the psalms.

So how does one go about learning something about shepherding images?

One of the best ways to start might be with a visit to a sheep farm to listen to what some people who raise sheep might have to say. For a person who has heard nothing but romantic and poetic interpretations of Psalm 23, such a visit can contain some pretty unsettling thoughts.

First, the question, "What are sheep really like?" brought a startlingly quick, emphatic, and definitive one-word answer, "Dumb!" And then, to soften his answer, the herdsman gave some everyday examples. He told how sheep might wander headfirst into a thicket and, without the help of the shepherd, would not have the common sense to simply back out and would remain stuck there until help arrives, or a predator, whichever came first. And the shepherd explained how sheep fear running water and will actually stand beside a bubbling fresh water stream and die of thirst unless the shepherd dips the water out for them to drink. And of course there were some humorous examples of sheep's well-known tendency to follow without question the lead sheep and the shepherd.

Somehow, although the shepherd's dedication and love for his sheep was unmistakable, none of the images ended up being very flattering when applied to the children of Israel or to the followers of Christ. Were any of these images really in David's mind as he penned Psalm 23? Could these images be referring to us?

Even with the most casual of readings one quickly spots the very traits the modern herdsman had described and it becomes very evident Psalm 23 could only have been written by one who truly knew and understood sheep. "Makes me

lie down in green pastures" and "leads me beside still waters" (RSV) are both descriptions of things a loving shepherd would know must be done to meet the needs of the sheep. Bubbling running waters were of no use to sheep and if the fields were full of snares and problems, the sheep would surely wander into them. The rod, the shepherd's weapon to defend the sheep, and the staff, the tool used to guide sheep, are all there. But did David really mean to imply and did Jesus really mean to say we, as people, are like sheep?

And what of all those wonderful romantic images of sheep as the frolicking symbols of innocence? After all, was not the innocence of sheep even a part of the Jewish sacrificial system? Not really. For the most part in the scriptures, lambs were symbolically innocent, not adult sheep. Jesus was the lamb of God, not the sheep. Sheep were—well, how can it be put nicely?— in need of a shepherd if they were going to manage life and survive at all. Sheep are almost totally dependent creatures and it seems almost everyone in biblical times recognized that trait. But are we really like sheep? Really?

The harder one studies the question the clearer the answer seems to be that Jesus truly is comparing us to sheep. Our human ability to get into whatever trouble there is to find in life and our need to be cared for, accepted, and loved are very much like the nature and character of sheep. No, this is not a very flattering view of humanity especially in an independence-oriented culture like the western world today. Being dependent is not an image of ourselves we want to hear. Nonetheless, our dependence upon Christ for our very existence is unmistakably stated in the scriptures.

But there is also a flattering side to all of this we have not yet mentioned. No matter how sheeplike we might be, the creator God of the entire universe loves us so much that Jesus came, lived among us, and died on the cross that we might get the message of God's love. It's true we were not very bright about receiving God's message. It's true nailing Jesus to the cross ranks right up there among some of the dumber moments in human history. But it is also still true God loves us so much the cross was worth going through if it would open our hearts to receiving divine love and salvation. We are pretty special sheep when you think about it.

In the late seventies at Springdale High School in Springdale, Arkansas, a special class of sophomores demonstrated the point. Juniors and seniors at SHS, with a full understanding of the implications, called sophomores "sheep." Calling sophomores "sheep" was a long-standing tradition and any sophomores who did not truly grasp the nature of sheep had it clearly explained to them. But then came this very special class of sophomores. They were bright and proud and not afraid to be who they were. At a pep assembly on Friday morning before an important football game that class of sophomores showed up wearing T-shirts emblazoned with large sparkling letters that read, "Super Shinin' Sheep." The juniors and seniors were beside themselves they were so upset and the more they tried to explain to the sophomores why this couldn't be done, the more the sophomores grinned and responded, "We may be sheep, but we are the very best sheep you ever did see!"

God's Super Shinin' Sheep. Maybe that's how we ought to think of ourselves. Rather than deny we might be like sheep, maybe we might celebrate that God, who knows us intimately, still loves us so much we have been gathered into one very special flock with our own divinely appointed Good Shepherd. Maybe rather than proclaiming our dignity, worth, and independence, we might better confess our shortcomings and sins and celebrate how we have been so incredibly blessed even to be included in the family of Christ. Maybe with a grin that comes only from a heart that has heard its master's voice say we are truly loved and forgiven, we ought to get ourselves some T-shirts with big fluffy sheep on them, and in large glittering words proclaim for all the world to see, "We are God's Super Shinin' Sheep!"

Prayer

Dear Lord, in a day and a culture that almost worships personal independence and self-reliance, it is sometimes very hard to hear your call for us to submit like sheep to your leadership as our Good Shepherd. Give us the strength, Lord, to reach out and entrust our lives to your care. Give us the wisdom to seek out and to follow your divine leadership rather than straying off in our own directions. Help each of us, Lord, to open our heart and accept your merciful restoring love. Through Christ our Lord we pray. Amen.

Midnight's Coming!

Imagine if you will, an apartment in one of our worst inner-city neighborhoods. It is not a nice neighborhood; in fact, it looks more like a war zone than a residential area. The apartment is small and dark and the building itself is in terrible condition. The hall outside the apartment door is dark and narrow and is filled with an odor one would think even the rats could not survive. When there is a light in the hall, it's only a 25-watt bulb, but most of the time the bulb has either been broken or stolen.

This is a tough violent neighborhood, and crime is a way of life here. Tensions are still high in this building after the tenant two doors down the hall was murdered only last night. There was no forced entry; the door had been unbolted from the inside. They don't use door bolts here like most might think. They have a large heavy bolt at the top and the bottom of the door and two heavy bolts in the middle so no one can force their way through.

It is a rainy dark evening and the day has really been cold. Of course, it almost goes without saying, the building heat is almost nonexistent, and the apartment is damp and cold.

Mrs. Jones lives here alone, and it is almost eight o'clock, the time she usually goes to bed on cold evenings to try to stay warm. Suddenly there is a knock at the door. Who could that be on such a nasty cold night? Should she risk opening the door or not?

WHO DO YOU SEE STANDING THERE IN THAT DARK HALLWAY KNOCKING ON MRS. JONES' DOOR?

Many good stories are word pictures, and like regular pictures, we each see something different in each of them. Often, we have our own preconceived ideas of what we are going to see in situations, and we are usually successful at fulfilling our preconceptions. Of those of us who allowed ourselves to picture in our minds the description of Mrs. Jones' apartment, probably no two of us saw Mrs. Jones the same way. No two of us saw the same door or the same hallway. In our minds we each were prepared to see things differently.

Just for the record, the person in our story standing in the hallway knocking on Mrs. Jones' door was a former gang member who became a Christian and is now an inner-city pastor there to visit and be sure Mrs. Jones was OK. Should she have opened the door? Of course! Was the pastor the person you expected in the hallway knocking at her door?

Parables are often like word pictures. But parables are usually meant to illustrate only one point. To focus on the lesser parts of a parable is to run the risk of missing the whole message it was meant to convey. For example, the intended message of the parable in today's passage is the wisdom of being prepared. If we focus only on the foolish maidens asking the wise maidens for oil and being refused, we may feel there was no Christian sharing going on here and thus miss the overall message entirely.

Let's take a moment to look at the symbols in this parable. Of course, we are the maidens—the people of Christ's church.

The wedding celebration is probably the purest symbol for unbridled joy—joy almost to a sense of abandon as families and communities celebrated this most special occasion.

Those who had oil were a symbol of those prepared for God's kingdom of love. Those who did not have oil symbolized those who would cling to being "religious" and live by the strictest letter of the law.

And what is "midnight"? For those unprepared, midnight was the darkest hour of the night. The time when all seems wrong and there seems to be not a glimmer of light or hope. On the other hand, for those who had oil and were prepared, midnight was the hour when the wonderful celebration and joy began.

Midnight can be the truest of tests of whether we have prepared our hearts before the Lord or not. Uell, for example, had worked hard all of his sixty years until one Lord's day afternoon he was stricken with a heart attack. For Uell and his family, midnight had come and certainly the hour seemed very dark. In that midnight hour, however, Uell's faith was being tested, and without fear he emerged from midnight into morning as a towering beacon of joy that remained his witness for the rest of his life.

Our midnight is coming. Whether it be the Lord's return or our own personal midnight, it is surely coming. Just as the way we were each preconditioned affected what we each saw in the word picture of Mrs. Jones, how we experience our midnight will depend a great deal on how we have prepared our hearts before the Lord. Will we be wise and prepared in our faith and receive great blessings and joy, or will we be foolish and caught empty and unprepared running in every direction, as the foolish maidens in our parable did, to see what oil we might find and miss the Lord's blessing? Faith building does not just happen; it requires work and development. And joy does not just happen; it comes when we have prepared our hearts for the Lord's presence.

Were your midnight to happen today, without warning, like Uell's did with his heart attack, which group of maidens would you be among? If the Lord were to return this week and the eternal celebration were to begin for all who were ready, would you be a part? Christ has personally invited each and every single one of us to be prepared and to be a part of the wedding celebration. In you heart today, how are you answering the Lord?

Prayer

Dear Lord, so often, like the maidens without oil, we have taken for granted we would always have time to prepare before midnight. We are so accustomed to the conveniences in life, we have sometimes forgotten we are also to be responsible. Take our hand, Lord, and walk with us and fill our lamps with oil. In Christ's name we pray. Amen.

Do You Love Me?

Call

This is the house of the Lord! Let all who have known God's mercy and grace be gathered this day, that the world might hear that the gospel of Christ is real!

Prayer

Dear Lord, as we gather today, draw us closer to you and open our hearts to a richer and fuller understanding of the call to service you have placed before us. God, so often we have taken your love for granted. Forgive us, and use us in whatever way you would choose. In Christ we pray. Amen.

Scripture

John 21:15-21

Hymns

"How Can We Name a Love"
"O Love That Wilt Not Let Me Go"

The theater is totally hushed as the heroine on the silver screen is breaking the tragic news to the handsome young man who has just saved the life of the movie's hero. "Chuck," she whispers softly as she moves very close where others will not hear. "I do love you, but not the way you're thinking. I love you like the brother I've always wished I had. My heart belongs to John. It always has, Chuck, and I'm sorry if you misunderstood, but it always will." With that she breaks away and returns to John's side who, strapped onto a litter, is being readied for transport to the hospital where he will recover fully and they will then be married and live happily ever after.

The word "love" has so many meanings today. You can love a person like a friend, like a parent, or like a spouse. We even use "love" to describe how we feel about our favorite food or activity. And we don't use any special prefixes to identify which meaning of "love" we are intending. Wouldn't it be easier if we said "a-love" means "I care about you like a friend." Then maybe "b-love" would be the romantic feelings we have for our mates. And "c-love" would be

34

the type of love we have for our parents. And finally, "d-love" is what we would call the feelings we might have for our favorite food or activity or objects of importance to us.

Obviously, all this silliness has only been an effort to make the point of how casually we use and overuse our word "love" in our everyday conversations. But other languages are not always so flexible with their word or words for "love" as we are in English. In fact New Testament Greek is so specific it uses several different words we would all translate into English as "love." If, for example, our movie heroine had been using words built on the Greek word *phileo* as she spoke of her feelings toward Chuck, he would have known all along she felt only a deep friendship or brotherly love toward him and not the sort of romantic or *eros* love she reserved only for John. Having several different words for "love" makes it easier to say what we really mean.

In our scripture passage today we have a very unusual conversation taking place between the resurrected Jesus and Peter. After breakfast, Jesus confronts Peter with what seems on the surface to be a very simple question. "Do you love me more than these?" In the last fifty to a hundred years a good deal of attention has been given to understanding exactly what Jesus meant by "more than these?" There does seem, however, to be something far more basic happening in this question we might want to consider first.

The Greek word for "love" the gospel of John records in the question Jesus places to Peter is based on *agapao,* or what we often use in the church today,

"agape." Agape is the highest form of love. This is an unconditional accepting love; it does not have a criteria attached suggesting, as a child might just before Christmas or a birthday, "If you give me what I want I will love you in return." Agape cares unconditionally for the other person. Jesus asks of Peter, "Do you love me more than these?"

Now Peter responds to Jesus, "Yes, Lord, you know that I love you." Did Peter answer the question directly? Not exactly. Peter did not use agape love in his answer; instead he used *phileo* love to describe how he felt about Jesus. In essence, Jesus questioned whether Peter had grown to the level of being able to walk with Jesus. Peter's answer was, "Jesus, I love you like a brother."

Peter did not fully respond to the question. Have you ever asked a teenager if he has all his homework done as he is sitting down to watch television and heard the answer, "It's under control." The answer does not fit the question, and a wise adult might well assume the true answer to be, "No, my homework is not finished but I want to watch this program." Jesus seems to understand full well what Peter is really saying and responds, "Tend my lambs."

Then for a second time Jesus poses the question, "Simon, son of John, do you agape love me? For a second time, Peter's answer does not directly correspond to the question as he tells Jesus again how he loves Jesus; Peter loves Jesus like a brother. Again, Jesus seems to truly understand what Peter is failing to say and commends him to be about the task of shepherding the young church.

Finally, for the third time, seemingly unable to draw Peter to the higher plane of agape love, Jesus restates the question, this time conceding and changing the tone completely as he asks Peter, "Do you love me like a brother?" Peter, unable to understand why Jesus has not accepted his two previous answers, responds to this third question, "Lord, you know all things and you know that I love you like a brother." Jesus must have smiled as for a third time he commends Peter to "tend my sheep."

There is such a beautiful image of the way the Lord loves each of us in this exchange with Peter. "Can you walk with me in love?" is the challenging question. Can we extend unconditional love freely as the Lord does to each one of us? Can we care about those who have nothing to offer in return? Do we love the Lord freely and without criteria, or do we love the Lord because we expect something in return like the child we spoke of expecting a nice Christmas or birthday present?

"Do you love me?" is a hard question! But even if our answer is like Peter's, "Yes, Lord, I love you like a brother who brings me great pleasure in our relationship." Jesus will love us, understand us, and walk side by side with us as we grow into the people the Lord intends for us to be. We hear Peter's answer in this scripture passage, but we also must remember the giant in the faith Peter grew to be before he gave his life in his Christian witness.

In our scripture today, Jesus stands before each one of us and asks, "Christian, do you love me?" If, from deep in your soul, you can add to your answer a total level of commitment, like Peter's, a commitment even unto death, and proclaim, "And Lord, no matter what circumstances in life may come, I am with you all the way!" then surely this day the Lord is pleased.

Prayer

Dear Lord, so often our faith is so small we really don't even understand the call you have placed on our lives. Touch us, Lord, and help us grow in your love. We know growth often comes through some pain, and we ask you to lead us through whatever it takes that we might one day say with joy in our hearts, "Lord we love you." It is in the holy name of Christ we pray. Amen.

Quiet Moments

Call

Let us come together in peace as we set the cares and concerns of everyday life aside. In the very depths of our souls, let us know that you are God.

Prayer

O Lord, you have blessed us with the privilege of coming into your presence; yet somehow we find the clutter and clamor of the world around us more appealing. Touch our hearts and let us hear your voice anew that we might share your word with a hurting world.

Scripture

Psalm 46:10

Hymns

"Be Still My Soul"
"Be Thou My Vision"

The world we live in is really a very noisy place. Often our day starts with an alarm or a radio jarring us out of the depths of sleep and into the mad rush of life. After we are up and going we then find ourselves amid the noises of the kitchen or of waking the children or maybe of preparing to whisk off to work. However we start the day, it is reasonably certain the remaining hours will most likely be filled with more and varied sources of noise. Even as we travel in the car with the radio off, we are surrounded by noises from the engine, road, and traffic so familiar to us we hardly notice them. If we add to all of the physical noises of life the attention-demanding voices of the people around us, we quickly begin to realize we live in a rather noise-filled environment.

But of course there is more. Whatever the level of the external noise in our life, we then must recognize we can have internal sources of interference as well—sources like our fears and anxieties and our worries and emotions. We can very well pressure ourselves at times when, for example, the deadlines of life play on our minds like legions of voices pulling in every direction. Or again we must consider the times when our worries about family or relationships virtually take our thoughts hostage, usually leaving us exhausted with little or nothing to show for it. And then we must also count the internal pressures we experience when life just seems terrible, such as the financially hard periods when we seem able to think of little else but how we are going to manage our bills and survive.

And if all that weren't enough, there is still the incredibly hectic pace of events in general we can set for ourselves. How often do we let ourselves get so involved in our projects and activities we come to the end of our day worn to a frazzle from running here and there doing this or that? Or how often have we let ourselves get stretched so thin, sometimes by church activities, that there is little emotional energy left for even ourselves, much less for us to share with our family and friends? And have you ever just crawled into bed at night so dead tired and exhausted you hardly remember pulling the covers up before you fell asleep? Life can be demanding.

And what about radio and television? How many of us, when we do have a moment to ourselves, are seldom without the sounds of either TV or a radio, or maybe even both, as we seek to fill the emptiness around us? Our world today is globally enmeshed by the wonders of modern mass communications and of course we have a social and cultural obligation to keep up with the news, don't we? Or how could we survive if we missed the very episode of our favorite soap that answered the question, "Did she or didn't she?" And surely we don't want to be the only person who missed the big game or the final episode of a top-rated sitcom.

Noise and distractions just seem to be an unavoidable part of living in these modern times. That's just how it is, right? How then, given the nature of our environment, can we possibly come to grips with the strange and almost incomprehensible words we read in the Psalms, "Be still, and know that I am God" (RSV).

Probably the first step in understanding God's call to us in Psalm 46:10 is to come to grips with the understanding that we have been divinely empowered to make choices in life. Most of the time we do what we want to do. Simply put, if our lives are hectic, demanding, and noisy, they are that way mostly because we make choices that keep us busy and overextended. Life is fast because we choose to set the pace of our lives so we are running at breakneck speed most of the time. By the way we invest our time we choose which activities and people we consider to be important. God created us as responsible beings, which means we have the power to make and live with our choices. This freedom of choice is a fundamental part of our created nature and, even if deep down we might suspect this to be true, we may still not want to admit it. Personal acceptance of this principle of responsibility could be costly. We might even be pushed to make changes in our everyday language. For example, common statements like "He makes me so angry!" might have to be rephrased into "I let him make me angry." Or "She makes me furious!" might be more honestly stated, "I let her make me furious." Whether or not our phrasing changes, because God has given us the power to choose, we must also understand we are responsible for the choices we make.

Would this principle say we could choose to be like Moses or Paul or one of the other spiritual giants in the scriptures? Only God has the answer to that question. But it might be interesting to remember the scriptures tell us both Moses and Paul chose to take time to get away and find quiet moments when they could commune with and listen to God. Moses pulled himself away from the incredible demands of leading a nation to climb a mountain and find a place where he could be still and meet God. Paul, the brilliant scholar, made the choice to find quiet times for God in his life. Only God knows the paths in life we would be set upon or the wonders we would see if we would only make the choice to find time for God in our life.

It all begins when we choose to find those quiet moments when, in a still small voice, God can speak to our heart. It begins when we will set the demands of the world aside and make room for time alone with God. It begins when we choose to let God be important enough to us that we invest some of our precious time in life in being alone with our Lord. Isn't it amazing? Marriages break up and friendships are lost when we get the message someone makes when they choose not to make time for us in their lives. Yet, somehow we seem to think God won't notice if we choose not to spend any time with God. It is probably safe to say God does get the message. Like a sad parent whose children are always too busy to ever get in touch, God hears the message of unimportance we are sending.

But there is good news! We make choices every minute of our lives, and we can make better choices. If you, in your heart today, are tired of the pounding noise of the world and are longing for an inner peace you just don't have; or if, in the depths of your soul you hear a ringing truth in the warning that you have been giving the wrong message of how important God is to you; or if you have had a gnawing feeling your life just isn't complete and you would like to meet and have God in your life today; then this is the time to commit your life to the Lord. And how do we build our relationship with God? Hear again God's voice through the Psalm, "Be still, and know that I am God." Start setting aside the quiet moments, and open your heart to Christ today.

Prayer

O God, give us the strength and the courage to let go of the noisy hectic world around us long enough to make time for you. Help us to understand, Lord, how much you love us and long to hear from us. Help us to accept your promise to always be there for us if we will simply make time for you in our lives. Thank you, Lord, for your love and your promise and all of the undeserved blessings you have already showered upon us. Through Christ we lift our prayer. Amen.

Little Tin Engine

Call

Let each of us who come this day to worship come bringing our total commitment to you, Lord, within our hearts.

Prayer

O God, you indeed can see even the most secret parts of our lives and you love us still. Today as we gather, help us to commit all that we are or have to you. Open our spiritual ears, Lord, that we might hear your call and know your voice. Through Christ we pray. Amen.

Scripture

Revelation 3:14-22

Hymns

"Take Up Thy Cross"
"Where He Leads Me"

The idea that being lukewarm is offensive to the Lord is to our current-day way of thinking sometimes a bit hard to understand. For many today, lukewarm seems like a comfortable temperature. Lukewarm is not bad as a sore throat gargle, and it can be a nice food temperature for one who has had recent dental work. There are lots of ways lukewarm can be useful when you think about it.

And the message that God would rather we be hot or cold only adds to the confusion. It is understandable that God would be pleased with our being hot, or as the old revivalists used to say, "On fire for the Lord," but what good is it if our hearts are cold or strongly against the gospel of Christ? Even lukewarm sounds better than cold.

But relationships are funny. Things are not always the way they seem. For example, if you were to walk into almost any Sunday school class and ask the question, "What is the opposite of love?" the most likely response you would get is "hate." But if you were to talk with experienced marriage counselors, you might well hear them describe couples who are doing emotional battle and seem to hate each other in very hopeful terms. On the other hand, these same marriage counselors might tell you the couples for whom they have the least hope are the ones who have given up on their marriage and just don't seem to care anymore. For couples without commitment there seems to be little left to work with.

And this is an important point in the dynamic of relationships. The opposite of love is not hate, for love and hate are both outgoing emotions. If we were to draw a circle to represent the basic person, the "me," then love might be an arrow pointed out from "me" in one direction and hate would be another outwardly pointed arrow from the "me" in a different direction. Both emotional arrows are pointed outward. But withdrawal or not caring about others would be represented by an arrow pointing inside the circle away from anyone and the rest of the world. Withdrawal or not caring is the true opposite of love.

Could this be what the Lord is trying to tell us in this passage about hot and cold and lukewarm? Could the spirit be telling us that genuine personal caring and commitment is what the Lord desires and withdrawal into our own self-centered uncaring apathetic little worlds is intolerable in the eyes of God?

The importance of our faith commitment is indeed the message our passage from Revelation has to share with us and the experience of the apostle Paul as recorded in the scriptures helps to confirm the point.

Anyone who has studied the scriptures most likely thinks of Paul as a sensitive, caring, dedicated, sincere, and intelligent person. There are some who would contend Paul was the most intelligent, gifted, and certainly the most highly educated of the New Testament authors.

But the apostle of love was not always so loving. Saul, as he was called then, was personally and sincerely committed to stopping the Christian movement. With the zeal of a fanatic, Saul sought to rid Judaism of what he saw as the terrible Christian blight. Saul was certainly not lukewarm, but rather he was frigidly cold toward the gospel of Christ as he struggled to be religiously perfect before God. Paul and his total dedication to his faith are a bit like a little tin engine an old model railroad enthusiast was showing the neighborhood children one day. The children had been watching in awe as the finely detailed model engines responded to the intricate directions of the old model railroader. Everything worked just like the real trains at the commands of a yardmaster. Then the old collector asked if they wanted to have some fun, and he brought out a very old little tin engine.

The little tin engine had none of the fancy details the newer models had and did not respond to the speed controls nor would it reverse directions like the sleek newer models would. All the little tin engine would do is go forward as fast and as hard as it knew how to go. When the old collector put it on the track the children had a wild time switching it away from the other trains and keeping it from having a collision. Everyone enjoyed the lively little engine and the challenge it gave them. But a couple of times the little tin engine got past the children's switching and was headed for a crash into another train. When it came too close, the old collector would always stretch across the model railroad board and, just in the nick of time, reach down and lift it off the track. With a smile he would place the little tin engine safely back on a piece of track where it could run wide open again like it was created to do.

In a way, that's how Paul was—going all out, like the little tin engine, holding nothing back in his commitment to doing the very best he knew how to do for the Lord. Then, on the road to Damascus, the Lord reached down and turned the totally committed Saul around and put Paul "back on track," giving us one of the greatest witnesses to the gospel of Christ the world has ever known.

The Lord is not afraid of sincere commitments in our faith, hot or cold; that is not the problem. But when we will not commit our lives and we will not reach out with all we have, this is a very different matter. Without commitment, we are lukewarm and we have no direction. Just as halfhearted and uncaring commitments are not acceptable in our human relationships, being halfhearted and uncommitted or lukewarm toward the Lord will not work either.

We have God's word that if we will put all we are into our relationship with Christ the rewards will be greater than we have ever dreamed. Unfortunately, many of us tend to know more about the latest TV programs, stock market closings, or our favorite athletic teams than we do of the scriptures or God's promises.

It is important to remember, however, we may not all have the same dramatic faith experience Paul had on the Damascus road. Instead, the Lord knows each one of us so personally our faith experience will be uniquely suited to who we are. It may be the Holy Spirit speaks to you in the depth of a quiet moment or maybe in experiences as spectacular as lightning or thunder. Either way it's our total commitment to Christ that is critical.

Fear not today. Commitment is the challenge. Get off of dead center and back to being full of life. It is not when we are hot or cold in our faith that is the enemy, but when we are lukewarm. Let each one of us today vow in our hearts to move forward from this place committed to taking our stand for Christ publicly, without shame, with all that we have, with all that we are, and in the best way we know how. Like the apostle Paul and Christians throughout the ages, we will not be lukewarm. We will stand tall and we will be known as Christians.

Prayer

Lord, give us the strength to trust you and to make our commitment today real. In the tough times and the times when some we once called friends might turn against us, help us to be true to you. Commitment is sometimes a bit scary and hard, Lord, but with your help, we can be faithful. In Christ we pray. Amen.

Abba

Call

Let us join together in worship all who would be a part of the family of God in Christ. Let our hearts bring forth praise through our words, our deeds, and our songs.

Prayer

O God, you have so richly blessed us through the Christ and your offer of adoption to all who would accept it. Lord, help us to know in our hearts the depth of love you hold for us and help us broaden our understanding of how wonderful your offer truly is. Through Christ our Lord we pray. Amen.

Scripture

Romans 8:14-17

Hymns

"Every Time I Feel the Spirit"
"Be Thou My Vision"

The English language, especially as we speak it on the North American continent, can be very difficult to learn. We use words so freely, and sometimes we use the same word to mean several different things. Try, for a moment, to think as a non-English speaking person might think trying to understand English. Think what you literally would hear if I were to say to you, "This work load is driving me up the wall!" Can you imagine how challenging this simple sentence might be as you try to figure out how some sort of "load" could be "driving" a person up a "wall." This sentence is full of common expressions we basically understand and take for granted but if someone takes these words literally, the sentence makes very little sense.

The words we use are important in determining how well the thoughts and images we are trying to convey are understood by those we intend to receive our message. Careful wording can mean clear communications. Children who have heard the stern aggravated voice of their parent call them emphatically by their first, middle, and last name know full well the clarity word choice can provide.

English is a living language: a living language in common everyday use. Common use, however, subjects word meanings to a constant process of change in order to meet the changing needs of modern living. A good example of this changing process is the word "cool." Once "cool" was used to indicate a thermal condition as in, "It is a cool evening," or to describe a reserved response such as, "They seemed rather cool toward the whole idea." Today "cool" has acquired additional uses such as in the phrase, "That's cool," implying something is good, or pretty much whatever the speaker wants it to mean.

And it is not just our word meanings that have been changing; we have been changing English grammar as well. But how important can all these changes be as long as we know what we are trying to say?

Let's try a little experiment. What do the words "thee" and "thou" mean, and what images do they convey to you as you hear them today? Everyone probably knows "thee" and "thou" are some archaic English forms of the word "you." But what are those archaic forms and what meaning were they intended to add for the listener? This is a difficult question, isn't it?

Although most of us have probably never thought about it, "thee" and "thou" are from the old "familiar" form in English that we basically no longer use. The role of the familiar was very special and we might understand it better if we see how it functions in other languages today.

German is a language still using the familiar. If a person calls a close friend on the telephone and asked, "Wie bist du?" they have simply asked "How are you?" If the response is the simple restatement, "Wie Sind Sie?" or "How are you?" the caller might as well hang up the phone. Both are translated exactly the same in English, "How are you?" The first, however, was in the familiar form reserved for only the closest of friendships, for parents, teachers, and God. The response was in the formal or polite form and by choosing the polite form, the caller was told their relationship is no longer close. So if we look again at "thee" and "thou," we might see they were once a part of our language that expressed closeness, warmth, and intimacy in relationships. Unfortunately, most of us no longer hear the warmth and intimacy of the familiar as we use these special forms today. Instead, "thee" and "thou" have become part of some special prayer language we use only when talking with God who might be offended if we were to pray using our everyday grammar.

What a cruel and twisted misconception to believe God might desire some special wording or that God might be offended by the ordinary grammar of our everyday language. The familiar we once used to convey God's desire to be close and intimate in everything we were about in life, through time, has become an enigmatic barrier holding us at arm's length from God's loving heart.

Does God really want to be that close and intimate with us? Do the scriptures truly support this view of God? Yes, it is true, and in our passage today Paul boldly declares God's love, but again the changing meanings of time try to mask it from us. In verse 8 Paul uses a term Jesus taught us we could use when talking to God, "Abba." We are privileged; no, actually, it is our inheritance by adoption to call God "Abba."

Why is it such a great privilege to call God "Abba"? The title "Abba" was the warmest and most intimate term a Jewish child used when speaking to a male parent. Our closest word for "Abba" today would probably be "Daddy," but how many of us can give ourselves permission to open our hearts and think of God, the almighty creator of the entire universe, as "Daddy"? Now we have located a serious problem. The barriers keeping God at arm's length are ours as we attempt to assure proper respect for God's majesty. This was exactly what the Pharisees were doing when they refused to say aloud the name of God for fear of saying it without proper respect. How ironic. Moses was given God's name to establish authority and closeness in Israel's relationship with God, yet with the passing of time the Jews grew fearful of speaking God's name, thus creating distance and separation.

Paul, however, boldly calls God "Abba" and shares with us how our relationship with God is not meant to be distant but rather like beloved children before the most loving parent one could possibly imagine. We are children before God and not like employees before an employer fearful of being fired.

What a difference words can make! They can make the difference of whether we hear the wonderful mystery of how indeed the very creator God of all the universe holds wide open a loving parent's arms ready to embrace us and to walk with us and talk with us in the most intimate and everyday terms we would like to use. But it is we who must open our hearts and minds and accept the gift of God's love. Words can make the difference between silence and communication.

Can you open your heart and mind and believe the testimony of Paul and the saints through the ages of God's incredible intimate love? Can you move beyond the worldly views of God as distant and aloof and risk returning home as did the prodigal to a loving parent God whose arms are wide open waiting to receive you? God's love seems too good to be true, but it's real and the decision of whether or not to accept it is ours today.

Prayer

Lord, sometimes we get so lost in the ways of everyday living that the gospel telling us of your love seems like more than we could ask for even in our wildest dreams. Take our hand, Lord, and receive our hearts today with all of the pain and sorrow we bring, and make us whole again. Give us the courage, Lord, to proclaim the reality of your love for all the world to hear. Through Christ our Lord we pray. Amen.

Loving God's Way

Call

Come, let all who would love God and serve your neighbor gather this day in worship before the Lord.

Prayer

Lord, help us to understand today your call that we should both love our neighbor and in a healthy way love ourselves. So often in the past we have been drawn to either love our neighbor or think only of ourselves when your commandment was truly to do both. Lead us to receive your love that we might truly love our neighbor. In Christ we pray. Amen.

Scripture

Mark 12:28-31; I Corinthians 13

Hymns

"The Gift of Love"
"Morning Glory, Starlit Sky"

It seems likely there are few verses besides John 3:16 that are more well known than the portion of Mark 12:31

saying, "You shall love your neighbor as yourself." It also seems probable there are few verses whose dynamic seems more demanding or is more frustrating and hard to understand than this verse. If you are like most of us, there have been times in your life when those people around us Jesus would have called our "neighbor" and worthy to be loved were, well to put it as politely as possible, some pretty hard to love folks. And moving in the other direction there are probably some among us who are far better at taking care of the smallest whim others might have while at the same time they fail to take care of even their most basic personal needs.

For generations it seemed most of the sermons we heard based on Mark 12:31 focused primarily on the part about loving our neighbor. And then, we seemed to swing the focus more toward the part about loving ourselves. Somehow, in the middle of all of this sermonizing, the whole concept of what it means to "love" seldom got much attention or explanation.

And then, to compound the confusion, there were those passages like Matthew 5:44 in which Jesus told us to be about the task of "loving" even our enemies. As if things weren't hard enough having to love messed-up neighbors whose property is a total eyesore lowering the property values for the whole community while they spend all their time swapping loud fishing stories every weekend with their friends over cases of beer, now we are also expected to like some character whose whole purpose in life is to do us in.

Not really! Actually the word "like" is never used in these passages. Jesus did not ask us to like our neighbor nor to like our enemy. The word Jesus did use was love, agape, and it does not mean like. We really do understand the difference between love and like.

Once in a weekend group focused on marriage enrichment, the very dynamic group leader enthusiastically asked, "How many of you love your marriage partner? Raise your hand." Without a moment's hesitation, hands went up all over the group. And then, after a dramatic pause through which the leader was obviously struggling for just the right timing and words, the leader turned and carefully restated the question as, "How many of you like your marriage partner?" There was a momentary pause and almost with an "Oops, I'd better get my hand up" expression on their faces the hands quickly went up. Like and love are not the same concepts today, and they were not in Jesus' day either.

What is agape love? To love my neighbor, my enemy, or myself I must understand what agape love is. Fortunately, the apostle Paul in the great love passage gave us some fantastic insights into agape. However, sometimes we might have to struggle with the language barrier a bit to come as close as we can to what Paul was really trying to share with us.

If we look at I Corinthians 13, we are likely to see all of those wonderful qualities of love most of us have heard about for years. "Love is patient" Paul tells us in verse 4. Time for a quick grammar lesson. In English, "love" is a noun and is the subject. "Is" is the verb. "Patient" is an adjective used as a predicate adjective, which means it follows the verb and describes the subject "love." All of this is traditional and very familiar to us, except in Paul's Greek wording there are no adjectives in this passage—only verbs.

No adjectives? No adjectives! A cumbersome way to translate this verse but probably much closer to the idea Paul was trying to convey might be, "Agape love is the act of choosing to be patient amid circumstances in which patience might not necessarily be the expected response"—the act of "choosing to be patient."

Or moving on to the next section—"Love is kind"—and it becomes "The act of choosing to be kind when circumstances would not necessarily dictate kindness." Choosing to be patient? Choosing to be kind? Hey, this is hard stuff Paul is telling us about.

How might we love ourselves in the light of this understanding of Paul's words? Say, for example, your best friend, who is also your neighbor, comes over for a glass of iced tea. Sitting at your kitchen table with one of those waterproof tablecloths on it, your neighbor accidentally knocks the glass over, spilling the tea. Would you jump up and immediately begin ranting and raving about what a dumb and stupid act this was? Probably not. Most likely your first thought and words would be not to worry about it while you clean things up and pour another glass.

Now, suppose instead of your friend spilling the tea, it was you. Now what would you be saying out loud and, maybe more importantly, to yourself? Would the temptation to call yourself clumsy and stupid be crossing your

mind or would you be extending the same love and patience to yourself you would have extended to your neighbor? This is hard work isn't it, but this truly is the understood meaning of how to love your neighbor as you love yourself that we hear Jesus telling us to be about in Mark 12:31.

And this exercising of your will in choosing patience and kindness and all of the other behaviors Paul lists for us in I Corinthians 13 are just as surely at the heart of what Jesus was commanding us to do when he said, "Love your enemy." There is no "liking" your neighbor necessary here nor are there any soft romantic notions in Paul's words defining agape love. Agape love is the mature intentional choice we can extend to others, even though they may not seem to deserve it. We are commanded to extend agape love to others, and we are just as surely commanded to extend it to ourselves.

But do we really have to do all of this? Love our neighbor? Love our enemy? Work at loving ourselves? Only if you would be called a follower of Christ; the choice is up to you.

Prayer

Dear Lord, help us recognize you accepted and loved us before we were truly able to understand what mercy and grace were. You reached out to us and even healed us during the very time the plans were being formed that would nail you to the cross. Forgive us, Lord, and give us the strength to honestly agape love our neighbor, our enemy, and ourselves that the world might know your love is real. In Christ's name we pray. Amen.

Good Neighbors

Call

Let all peoples from every nation who would seek to serve the Lord gather this day and worship!

Prayer

Dear Lord, as we gather together today, touch our hearts with a new awareness of what it means to be a good neighbor. Call us afresh to walk where you would have us to walk and to give help, healing, and love without judgment or condemnation to all you would place in our path. Through Christ our Lord we pray. Amen.

Scripture

Luke 10:25-42

Hymns

"Jesus' Hands Were Kind Hands"
"O Jesus, I Have Promised"

The story of the Good Samaritan has challenged the hearts and minds of almost everyone in the church since the time Jesus first gave it to us. Every facet of this story seems aimed at any self-righteousness that might exist in the church. The setting within which Jesus tells us about the Good Samaritan and even the identity of the story's characters all add to its message.

First, let's look at the setting. An obviously devout lawyer approaches Jesus with what was potentially an entrapping question about what one should do to inherit eternal life. The word "lawyer" here does not refer to an expert in the laws of the land—after all this was a period of Roman rule—but rather to an expert in the laws of Moses and how they related to God's chosen people. During the time of Jesus' ministry the debate was still raging between the Pharisees, who believed in life after death, and the Sadducees, who did not believe in life after death. But the lawyer's question went beyond this issue and contained within it a test to determine how orthodox the teachings of Jesus were.

The response Jesus gives is nothing short of brilliant. With finesse Jesus implies the truth of eternal life and then draws out of the lawyer the Mosaic Laws on the subject. How could Jesus be a wild-eyed radical to be feared if all he was teaching were the laws of Moses?

But the lawyer is sharp, and the exchange does not end here. The lawyer asks a follow-up question seeking further clarification as he pushes Jesus to define "neighbor." Seeking a specific definition would have been an instinctive act for the lawyer. The religious leadership of the day had codified in minute detail almost every function of daily life. Volumes and volumes had been written by the time Jesus was attempting to clarify the law. Several books sought to interpret and explain the Sabbath law alone. The lawyer, who believed the law was given exclusively for God's people, was seeking to learn if Jesus was using the acceptable meaning of the term "neighbor" as referring to one of God's chosen, a Jew who lived nearby, or if Jesus held to some radical and unacceptable use of the word?

Again the answer Jesus gives by telling of the Good Samaritan is nothing short of brilliant. The characters in the story, however, must surely have been quite shocking to the lawyer.

The story opens with a man traveling from Jerusalem on the road to Jericho. It is probably a safe assumption that those hearing Jesus tell the story saw the traveler as a Jew. The traveler, through no stated fault of his own, is beset upon, robbed, and badly beaten by thieves who leave him for dead along the road. Next, Jesus makes a strong point as he tells of the three people who happen upon the victim.

The first person to find the victimized traveler is a priest. The priest is a symbol of the religious system in the temple. The laws of purity that the priest must live by prevented him from even touching a dead body lest he become impure and no longer be able to carry out his priestly functions until complete purification had been accomplished. Thus, the priest was too religious and too holy to get involved with this victimized child of God, so he continues on his way as a holy spiritual leader among the faithful.

Along comes the second person who finds the battered traveler by the road. The second person is a Levite. The Levites were devout members of the temple community that maintained the facilities and cared for the symbols of the faith. Again, the Levite did not want to become involved with this hopeless battered creature, so he moved over to the other side and passed on.

Today, the actions of these two religious leaders seem to us a bit cold and callous. Again, we have to remember the theology of Jesus' day believed that bad things happened to bad people and good things happened to good people. Jesus often confronted and challenged this belief because it was so widely held. In the eyes of the priest and the Levite, the victim was probably only receiving the just rewards for his own sin and deserved whatever punishment God had wrought upon him. Furthermore, why should either of them question the wisdom of God, or, for that matter, why should either of them interfere with God's punishment?

Now, the Samaritan comes along. Who is a Samaritan? After the death of Soloman, the kingdom of Israel split. The half to the north became known as Israel and the part to the south Judah. Eventually Samaria became the capital of Israel and by the time of Jesus the kingdom was known as Samaria. After Israel had been conquered by the Assyrians and the period of the Babylonian captivity, the Jews considered the Samaritans so corrupted and impure as to be totally unacceptable as a people. The lack of tolerance that exists today between many Jews and Arabs is probably no less severe or bitter than existed between the Jews and Samaritans in Jesus' day.

But it is the Samaritan who finally comes along and tends to the needs of the wounded Jew. It is the Samaritan who displays compassion and sees to it the Jew gets the care and treatment he needs to recover. It is the Samaritan who opens his purse and provides the traditional desert hospitality to one traveling in need without asking any questions. It is the unacceptable Samaritan, and not the priest or the Levite, who ultimately did exactly what Jesus led the lawyer into stating was required to be done if one was to receive the eternal life the lawyer had presumed was reserved exclusively for the chosen Jews.

This had to be a shocking story for the devout Mosaic lawyer to hear from Jesus. For that matter, the lesson of the Good Samaritan can be just as threatening today if we are inclined to seek our personal safety within the walls of the church as we ignore the battered hurting world beyond the church doors. How many of us have ever traveled to church and passed by "those less fortunate" and breathed a sigh of relief we are not living like they are? How many of us have seen our neighbor, maybe a struggling wounded single parent in our midst, and we have been critical rather than finding ways to help? Or how many of us have spent hours and hours gift shopping and working on cantatas for a special sea-sonal worship service, but we have been too busy to get by to see that elderly shut-in we know who has no family left to care for her?

The words of Jesus are penetrating. If we are truly committed to following Christ, we must be about loving our neighbors, whoever they may be and from whatever background they may have come. The warning is clear. Eternal life does not belong to those who are simply being religious or holy, and this is not what the true followers of Christ are about. Instead, we are called to be living witnesses of Christ's love; we are called to be good neighbors.

Prayer

Lord, give us the vision to see and the ability to hear the cries of those in need around us, and give us the courage to get involved and help. Carrying your love into the world involves some risk and hard work, but the reward, if we will be faithful, is eternity. Thank you, Lord. In Jesus' holy name we lift our prayer. Amen.

Sin Is Sin

Call

Let each who has sinned and fallen short of the glory of God come together and give praise for God's loving mercy and grace.

Prayer

O God, so often we look beyond our own sins and critically judge the sins of others. And Lord, sometimes we see our sins as unforgivable while we quickly proclaim your mercy and willingness to forgive the sins of others. Through your grace, Lord, let us realize that even though we are sinners, we are forgiven and made clean through the cross of Christ. Hear our prayer, O Lord. Amen.

Scripture

Romans 3:22-27; Matthew 7:1-5

Hymns

"Rock of Ages"
"There's Within My Heart a Melody"

A titter floated across the sanctuary as Samantha came in with her almost newborn son.

Sam had literally grown up in the church, making her own first visits to the nursery within a week after she was born. Until she was a sophomore in high school, Sam had participated in virtually every children and youth function the church had held. Somehow that all ended, however, when, at the beginning of her junior year, Sam announced to her family and the world that she was old enough to make up her own mind now and she no longer wished to be a part of that naive crowd down at the church.

Only a short time later Sam learned that she was pregnant. Not being married, this was the most difficult problem she had ever faced and at first she felt she would have to face it all alone. There were hours of heartbreaking tears and agony. At one point she even considered taking her parent's car and running it off a cliff to end it all. But she knew that was no solution.

Then came the agonizing task of telling everyone what was happening. One evening, as they sat together in the car on the way to a movie, Sam blurted out the truth to the baby's father. Her boyfriend flinched in shock, and then with a tone of obligation, offered to marry her. To her credit, Sam told the young man she appreciated his offer, but she would have to think about marriage for a while. Although he promised to stay in touch and help out with expenses, that was the last Sam saw of the young man.

Now came an even harder task. How could Sam tell her family what had happened after she had said all the things she had said to them. It took all the courage she could summon up to call the pastor, whom she had trusted as a friend for as long as she could remember. Maybe somehow the pastor could help. Maybe, Sam wished, there really are miracles and maybe somehow the pastor would show her a way to make things right again.

But the pastor had no simple answers. Much to her relief, however, the pastor did not give her a "We told you so" speech. Instead he listened intently to Sam's every word and, when she broke down in tears, hugged her, and assured her that she was not the first to make a mistake, and that she was not alone. Sam's entire church family would be behind her and would help in any way they could. With those words Sam almost exploded in tears; only this time there were the tears of joy. Sam was experiencing the joy that only a ray of hope in what seems like total darkness can bring.

The meeting with Sam's parents was just as emotional as the meeting with the pastor. Sam was overwhelmed by the love and support she felt from her parents. Indeed her parents behaved like the father of the prodigal son rather than the nagging, complaining critics Sam had envisioned they would be. It would not be easy for Sam to manage having a child and finishing high school, but the support of her family gave her the strength to try.

Now it was her first time back in church since the birth of her son. A small handful of people in the congregation wondered how Sam could have the nerve to come back now. A smaller number considered Sam to be unfit to be in God's house. The vast majority of the members, however, shared a prayer of celebration. It was as if one big family had just had another grandchild. It was a very special day when Sam brought her baby to the nursery for the first time. Actually, Grandma, Grandpa, and Mom brought little Adam and there were no prouder people in the whole world that day as everyone oohed and aahed over the third generation to attend the church.

In the months between Sam's dramatic announcement and the birth of Adam, Sam felt she learned more about true life and the message of Christ than she had learned during all her years in Sunday school. In an impromptu but loving conversation with Ellie, one of her early Sunday school teachers, Sam wondered out loud how the church could have welcomed her back so openly. Ellie smiled broadly and put her arm around Sam as she said, "Sam honey, we're all sinners in this church. We've all made our mistakes in life and know the Lord will forgive 'em. How could we not forgive yours, child?" "But I messed up so badly," Sam protested. "Sin's sin, girl! There are no big sins and little sins in God's eyes. And like I said, most all of us in this church are sinners."

There have been a lot of changes in that community over the past twenty years. Sam graduated from high school and married a year later. Several of the wise and loving generation who had the wisdom to welcome her with open and loving arms when she needed them are now with the Lord. You can be assured of one thing, however. As long as Sam and those like her who had heard firsthand about the mercy and grace of the Lord are alive and at that little church, the gospel of Christ will be heard through the love and openness of its members.

Prayer

Dear God, thank you for loving us so much you paid the price that we all might be forgiven and welcome in your kingdom. Through Christ our Lord we pray. Amen.

What If?

Call

Let all who would celebrate the return of the Lord gather together this day to worship with praise in their hearts.

Prayer

Lord, touch our hearts today with the courage to believe your day of return will one day come. So often the ways of the world would have us believe you are not God, you do not care, and you will not return. Receive the celebration from our hearts today as we give you praise that your love and mercy are real. In Christ we pray. Amen.

Scripture

Mark 13:24-37

Hymns

"O Day of God, Draw Nigh"
"I Surrender All"

What if tomorrow your household received a letter in the mailbox after the regular mail had already come? With no special reason in mind, you just felt compelled to check your mail again and there it is, this letter addressed to your family. It has no stamp on it, just a cross where the stamp should be. It has no return address, just your address on the front. So you open it and inside you find this short note:

Dear (your family name),

Next Sunday I will be returning to see and be with all of you. I have so longed to join you again, and I will be bringing all who are ready home with me.

I will see you then,

Your loving brother,

Jesus

You look at this letter and at first you are annoyed. You figure it is some sort of prank or practical joke. Then you decide this isn't funny, and you are going to do something about it! It is time for a few phone calls to the proper authorities!

So it's off to the phone you go and with every step you get more furious. Then you try to dial and the lines to the police and the post office are all busy. This situation is becoming very strange.

Next you decide to try calling the church, and we are not sure what is going on either. All we know is that we got one of the letters too. It's beginning to look like a lot of folks in the area got this note. Well, there isn't much left to do, so you decide to forget it.

A little later in the evening you turn on the television to watch the news. Sure enough the lead story is all about the letters that have mysteriously appeared wherever Christians live or work, always in the native language, all over the world. The letters all say the same thing, and heads of state everywhere are wondering what is happening.

Suddenly you and Christians everywhere begin to wonder if this could be for real. Now one line in the letter begins to stand out as being very important. "I have so longed to join you again, and I will be bringing all who are ready home with me." After rereading the letter over and over, everyone is starting to realize there are some important things that need to be done.

There is the man who hadn't spoken to his brother in twenty years. After reading the letter he gets into his car and drives over to his brother's house to work things out.

There is that couple involved in an extramarital affair they knew was wrong from the very beginning. They have to talk and get their lives and marriages back in order.

There is the lady who is so angry at some of the other ladies in her social club she has vowed in her heart to get revenge whatever it takes. Now she just wants to get things straightened out and end the bitterness.

There is also the family with the plans to leave for their second European vacation this year, even though they never seem to have the time to call or get by to visit with either set of parents. After the letter the second vacation plans don't seem that important.

Or what about the folks who suddenly telephone the church wanting to know how they might be able to "catch up a little on their giving."

And then there is the church committee (across town of course) that had been feuding over who was going to have the final say on whether or not the pastor would receive some time off. Suddenly the phones are ringing and an emergency meeting of the committee is called. To the surprise of no one, the committee votes to give the pastor a three-day study leave.

And how about the local business that had kept a dual set of books for years suddenly calling the IRS requesting the chance to come clean and voluntarily pay up their taxes.

And so it goes on and on as people realize the day of final accounting is at hand and the Lord's return is imminent.

It is fairly certain this mysterious letter from Jesus will probably never happen, not because the Lord is not coming, but because we have already been given all the notice we are going to get. Be assured, however, Christ is coming again and make no mistake, we most likely will have no more warning when that time comes, than our mysterious letter would have given, and it's doubtful we will have that much. Or then again if you think about it, death could call us home at any time with no warning at all.

It is doubtful there is a pastor anywhere who has not heard many times a list of regrets while visiting bereaved families. Regrets for the things we wish we would have said or the little things we wish we would have done to let the loved ones, now gone, know how much we loved them. Silly arguments we wish we would have never carried on and taken so seriously. Times when a hand could have been held one last time or a good-bye kiss given as a loved one went out the door to go to work. But who could have known death would come?

So the real question becomes: *Are we living the way we want to be living should either Christ return today or our time on earth suddenly come to an end?*

Only you can answer this question. Only you know the areas of your life you would be uncomfortable talking to Jesus about face to face. Only you know the relationships in need of mending or the value systems in need of change. Only you know the apologies that need to be made or the wrongs that need to be righted.

The good news is that we do have today. We have the time and the chance to make whatever changes and commitments we need to be prepared to stand before the Lord. Praise God, we have this day! What changes and commitments do you need to make as we look forward to being in the presence of Christ?

Lord, sometimes we get so involved with the hectic pace of modern living that we lose track of you and what you taught us was important. Help us to keep our focus on you, God, that we might be able to see the areas in our life in need of change to make ourselves ready for your return. We praise you, Lord, for giving us this wonderful day in which to serve you. In Christ's name we pray. Amen.

Thinking About Jeremiah

Call

Come, let all who would seek the word of the Lord and proclaim Christ to every nation gather and worship this day.

Prayer

Dear Lord, help us to bring the thoughts of our hearts back to how you would have us serve without questioning your use of the results of our efforts. We are called to be witnesses of your love, and we give you praise and honor for your mercy and your grace in our lives. Through Christ our Lord we pray. Amen.

Scripture

Jeremiah 12:1-6

Hymns

"Give Me the Faith Which Can Remove"
"How Firm a Foundation"

Brad had worked hard to prepare for the district track meet and now the start of the four hundred, his best race, was only minutes away. All through the spring track season Brad had finished no worse than second in his high school conference and he felt prepared today to run the best race he had ever run. In all probability, less than half a second would determine the difference between first and third place in this race.

It is amazing the thoughts that can race through a person's mind in the final few seconds before a race. Of course Brad already knew exactly the strategy he planned to use, but the four hundred is pretty much a flat-out sprint race. But Brad also had a sense of purpose beyond the race itself. The year before, he and several of the other athletes started a Bible study at school, and he really wanted to prove that people who take serving the Lord seriously can be winners. Looking almost totally preoccupied as he took his lane, Brad was talking to the Lord about using this race to somehow bring honor to Christ.

Totally focused now on his lane assignment as all the race contestants set up for the staggered start, Brad heard the starter call, "On your mark!" Only a few heartbeats later the gun sounded and the eight fastest runners in the four hundred were pouring every ounce of strength they had into a record setting pace around the track. Much less than a minute later Brad crossed the finish line a second behind a runner he had beaten in every previous meet that spring by more than three tenths of a second. How could this be happening? It just wasn't possible.

Still gasping for breath and managing to summon up a smile, Brad reached out his hand to congratulate the young man who came in first as all the runners were being sorted out by their finish order and escorted over to the officials. In his heart Brad was whispering to the Lord how he would accept the way the race came out and asked God to use even his second place to somehow honor Christ.

On the long bus ride home, however, things changed. It was on the bus that Brad learned from one of the pole vaulters who had been talking to a vaulter from the same school as the winner of the four hundred how their four-hundred runners had been experimenting with some special pills shortly before the last few races of the season— pills that had never been detected in any high school drug screens but that seemed to better the runners' times.

Brad was upset by the idea the runner who beat him in the four hundred might have used chemicals to win. How could God have let such a thing happen? How many times had Brad read in the scriptures that God would not let the ways of the unrighteous prosper, yet here clearly it seemed a person who may very well have violated the whole spirit of fair and honest competition, had walked off with the gold medal as a testimony to doing anything it takes to win. "It's not right, God!" Brad's inner voice cried out to the Lord.

At the Bible study the following week, one of Brad's friends used the concor-dance in the back of his Bible to try to find a passage that might provide some understanding and guidance for Brad. They decided to try Jeremiah 12:5 and see what it had to say.

The twelfth chapter of the book of Jeremiah opens with Jeremiah, like Brad, complaining to God about how the wicked seem to be doing just fine while he, an obedient prophet of God, is receiving no respect at all and having to fend for his life. Verse five begins God's reply to the prophet by posing the question back to Jeremiah that if he is having trouble running the race against regular footmen, what will Jeremiah do when God matches him against horses? And if this did not make the point clearly enough, God continues by pointing out that if Jeremiah is stumbling and having trouble running in the open territory, what will Jeremiah do when God places him to run in the wilderness?

The words in verses five and six cut through Brad like a knife. He had never realized his kinship with a biblical personality as clearly as he did at that moment with Jeremiah. Just like Jeremiah, Brad was complaining about how the people who do not play by the rules seem to be winning and God was challenging Brad to consider if he thought things were bad now, how would Brad feel when matters became more difficult as it seemed God was implying they were certainly going to become?

Ultimately, Brad knew in his heart the real question he had to answer was, "Who is really in charge of my life, God or myself?" There was no question, really; God is in charge. As soon as he arrived at the understanding that God truly was in charge, Bard felt his peace and confidence return. Even though he could not explain why things happened the way they did, Brad believed and trusted God had everything under control. Brad knew in his heart that in the overall scheme of God's plan somehow everything would all work out for the best. All Brad was responsible for doing was being faithful in his personal walk before the Lord, and the rest was up to God.

And how many of us at one time or another have found ourselves like Jeremiah and Brad, fussing at God for things not going the way we know they should? Do we fuss because the wrong people seem to be prospering while the honest and loving people are struggling just to keep their heads above the water? Probably most of us at one time or another have, whether we realized it or not, been brothers and sisters in spirit to Jeremiah.

But surely we must also hear God's challenge to Jeremiah and to those who would spend their time complaining about the mission the Lord has laid before us. If we think things are bad now, how will we manage when the Lord puts us up against the really difficult tasks ahead? Would God match us against even more challenging missions? The scripture text in our passage implies God has every confidence in those who have been chosen to serve. Furthermore, verse five suggests God fully intends to send the faithful, even those who complain, on to harder battles, not as punishment, but to demonstrate it is God's power, not ours, which will carry out the battles and it will be to God the ultimate victory belongs.

Somehow there can be a warmth and a comfort in knowing even the prophets complained at times to the Lord. Jeremiah's openness encourages us to be open and honest with God about all that we feel and think. But we must also be prepared to hear God's challenge to Jeremiah and God's challenge to us that we might grow in our faith and soar with the eagles as we learn to allow the power of the Lord to be our standard and our guide.

Prayer

Dear Lord, thank you for allowing us to complain sometimes, and still having the confidence in us to push us on to ever greater tasks. We love you for the patience and mercy you have already given us, Lord. Lead us on now into greater missions. Through Christ we pray. Amen.

They Knew All Along

Call

Come, let believers of every age come together and worship that we might share in the glory of the Lord.

Prayer

Dear Lord, help us to grow in faith and wisdom that we might be the witnessing church you have called the body of

Christ to be. Through Christ our Lord we pray. Amen.

Scripture

Titus 2:1-15

Hymns

"Filled with the Spirit's Power"
"Lord, Speak to Me"

Shena's favorite person in the whole world to visit and talk with was her grandmother. Gram lived only about three blocks away, and there were many days Shena would go to Gram's after school until her own parents came home from work.

Gram looked forward to Shena's visits and almost always had some homemade treat ready for Shena when she arrived after school. When Shena stayed overnight, Gram never failed to tuck her into bed with a Bible story told only the way Gram could tell it.

Shena grew up in the presence of her Gram's everyday witness of how God and Jesus were not just names on a printed page to be studied, but personal friends who Gram talked with and shared every little thing in life. When Shena had a problem, she and Gram could sit down and talk about it and then Gram would tell her, "Give me your hand child. Now let's tell Jesus all about it." Shena grew up talking to Jesus about almost everything in her life, because Gram showed her that was the best way to live.

When Shena was twelve, her parents felt she ought to be in Sunday school somewhere so they decided to start going to church. It was hard for Shena to understand why all of the folks Gram's age were in their own class and not with the young people like herself. Shena loved Sunday school and soon became a favorite of her classmates and her teacher as she enriched and vitalized the Bible stories in a way only a person who knows and loves the Lord can do, just as her Gram had done for her. Is it any wonder Shena has maintained her close personal relationship with the Lord or that today she is in full-time Christian ministry?

Robert was in his second year of seminary when he had the opportunity to pastor a small congregation in an agrarian community about forty miles away from the campus. Like so many of the farming communities in the area, many of the younger generation had moved into the city where work was more available for them. As a result, the little church Robert was going to serve had more people in the senior generations than in the younger ones.

After about a month in his new church setting, the senior adult Sunday school class asked Robert if he would teach their class for a quarter. Robert agreed and an adventure Robert would never forget began.

Through the week Robert worked hard at his seminary studies and, as is so often the case, gained many new insights about life he had never really considered before. Part of his new insights may have been from his studies, and part of them may have come from the experience of maturing; the two can be hard to separate at times. Robert was usually excited as he arrived at the church and shared his latest bit of newly acquired wisdom with the Sunday school class.

Robert had fallen in love with the people in his senior adult Sunday school and it was obvious the feeling was mutual. Never did Robert approach teaching the class as if he were the ultimate source of God's wisdom, but more as an excited believer anxious to share with good friends a wonderful pearl of wisdom the Lord had provided during the past week. The class could sense his spirit and loved Robert all the more for his openness.

One Sunday morning in class Robert had been particularly excited about the lesson he had prepared to teach. About halfway through the class time Robert was halted in his tracks by the looks he suddenly realized were on the faces of the class members. The class members were smiling at him with their eyes. When he thought about it, the smiles had been there from the first day Robert had taught the class. In that instant Robert realized these wonderful mature Christians knew all along the jewels of wisdom he had so excitedly been bringing before them each week.

Seeing his hesitation, someone asked if he was all right. Robert said he was and with a deep, long breath set his lesson aside and asked if he could visit with the class for a moment. "Sure," came the answer. "What seems to be the problem?"

What happened next totally changed Robert's theology. He asked them if they did not already know most of what he had been so excited about teaching them. The class admitted that indeed they were pretty much familiar with most of what he had been teaching. "Why didn't you tell me you already knew these things instead of letting me

go on and on up here?" Robert asked. "Because we love to hear the gospel and to see another generation come to love it as much as we do," they replied.

In that simple final answer, Robert came face to face with reality. The gospel of Christ is not conveyed only by well-trained seminary scholars who had poured over great theological volumes for years and years. It is also conveyed by people who lived their faith from sun up to sun down like these very people sitting before him in the Sunday school class. Robert would share later that at that moment his heart almost burst with joy, and he gladly resumed sharing his latest insights with these wonderful people who knew them full well.

Certainly as Christians we are charged to study and show ourselves approved before the Lord. But we are also charged to live our faith in a real and open way so as to share the good news by our very lives for each generation to see. For nearly two thousand years, the gospel has been passed on from generation to generation and for much of that time the good news was shared without the benefit of affordable scriptures everyone could own and study for themselves. Let us each one personally remember, even beyond the printed page, a Christian life is a most powerful and resounding witness for the Lord.

Prayer

Dear Lord, help us remember how the world will hear the good news through our lives more clearly than it will through our words. Use us, Lord, to faithfully carry the gospel to all of the generations in every land. In Christ we pray. Amen.

There Ain't No More Tomorrows

Call

Come into the house of the Lord all who would this day lift your voices in song and praise before the Lord God Almighty.

Prayer

O God, so often we have sought after the things of the world and forgotten our commitment to serve the risen Christ. Help us today to hear your call to stand firm in our faith for all the world to witness. In Christ we pray. Amen.

Scripture

Luke 12:13-21

Hymns

"Give of Your Best to the Master"
"Whom Shall I Send?"

Todd was asked to share at the Saturday evening session of the weekend spiritual retreat some portion of his personal faith pilgrimage. Todd was in his late thirties and in the eyes of most who had known him over the past ten years, he was a relatively successful person. Todd was one of those people who seldom sought recognition but who was often called upon to lead a group or a task force. Most felt Todd to be responsible, fair, and willing to work hard at whatever task had to be done.

This particular retreat was originally planned to be especially for Christian business people, but, as it turned out, everyone who expressed an interest was encouraged to attend. That Saturday evening Todd was standing before business people, housewives, educators, graduate students, a postal employee, people who worked in the construction trades, and an auto mechanic. It seemed the only thing this group had in common was its love for Christ.

Todd opened his message by sharing a little about his background. He grew up in a fairly solid middle-class home with both parents very involved in the family business. Todd's mother and father were also very involved in the lives of their three children. It did not matter whether it was PTA or Scouting, one or both of Todd's parents would be there to support it.

During Todd's grade school years, his parents were so supportive that Todd became a little annoyed with them at times. There were occasions when his parents disagreed with some of the policies where Todd went to school and would become personally involved in whatever efforts were necessary to accomplish the desired changes. Todd saw his parents as never being willing to just let well enough alone, but when they felt conditions needed attention, they would meddle and get involved to see what could be done.

Through his college years, however, Todd began to grow very close to his family, especially his parents, and he became accustomed to discussing almost anything he felt was important with them. Any topic was fair game from politics to his personal life, and Todd really began to understand and value something his father taught him. Todd's father used to tell him there was no problem Todd could get into that someone had not already been through and would be willing to help with if only Todd had the courage to open up and seek help.

As the last rays of the setting summer sun were fading in the window behind him, Todd shared how he had allowed himself to grow comfortable with life in general. He worked hard and made a reasonable living and seldom got involved with the problems of the world around him. As a child Todd had seen the stresses and strains his parents had gone through battling the problems in life, and after college he pretty much felt he would focus on taking care of his own home and leave the battles to be fought by his parents' generation. If he thought about being involved, it was always in the future.

But one day about ten years before the spiritual retreat, a major change came in Todd's life. His father experienced a serious heart attack and eventually died. Todd remembered how a few weeks after his father's funeral he had been outside working on a sunny cold February day when the Lord began to help him understand it was time for Todd to put away his childish ways and to become more responsible for matters in the world around him. As Todd walked in the silence of the bright winter sunshine, he felt the presence of the Lord as he had seldom experienced it before. Todd felt as if he were seeing again all of the times when he had walked away from his responsibilities and the times when he had let serious matters and even the

little odd jobs around the house he had been asked to do go until a "tomorrow" that seldom ever came. Todd shared how he felt the Lord had given him a little slogan to remember, "There ain't no more tomorrows."

It didn't matter if it were grammatically correct or not, Todd had never shared it with anyone before anyway. It was a personal slogan vaguely based on something Todd had often humorously said to himself when he had found himself in difficult times before the death of his father. Todd felt the Lord was showing him the best time to do something was when the Lord opened the door of opportunity for a person to do it. The best time to work, the best time to play, the best time to minister to others, and the best time to take care of your own health and get your needed rest were all as the Lord opened the way. For Todd, when he was tempted to put off something he should be getting accomplished until another day, he would simply repeat the little slogan the Lord had given him, "There ain't no more tomorrows."

In the discussion that followed Todd's sharing, a retired businessman related a particularly poignant story. He and his wife of many years had worked very hard, never taking any time away from their business so they could save their money for their retirement years. Shortly after they had retired and finally began to make plans to enjoy the life they had sacrificed so long to make possible, his wife was discovered to have inoperable cancer and within three very painful months was dead. With tears in his eyes he lovingly suggested to those young enough to still be in the active work force to value their loved ones and make time for them while they have it, for as

Todd had already suggested, no one has any guarantee there will be a tomorrow.

Then one of the educators spoke up and shared how the Lord seemed to be calling him to stop by and visit a neighbor and share the gospel. This calling had been on the educator's heart for several weeks. One afternoon as he was passing the neighbor's house, the neighbor was in the yard washing her car. The educator knew he ought to stop but he was tired and it being Friday he made a promise to himself and to God he would get by to see the neighbor tomorrow. Within the hour after the educator had seen the neighbor washing her car the neighbor was killed in a terrible automobile accident. For the educator and his planned visit to share the gospel with the neighbor there were no more tomorrows.

Almost all Christians have a confession of a time when they let pass an opportunity for ministry for one reason or another only to find the door closed forever. The next time we feel the Lord tugging at our hearts to minister to one of God's beloved sheep and we are tempted to wait or to leave it until another time, let us try to remember how the rich man in our scripture passage died without warning, or how each of the shared experiences at the retreat echo the call to be faithful in the day that we have. If it will help, we might even remind ourselves of Todd's streetwise slogan, "There ain't no more tomorrows," and be assured God is far more concerned about the love in our heart for those in the world around us than the grammar of our inspirational slogans.

Prayer

Dear Lord, thank you for caring so much you even speak to us in the ways we hear you best. Help us to realize today is all we have and help us to remember when we are tempted to put off those things you would have us be doing today that we have no guarantee there will be any tomorrows. In Christ we pray. Amen.

Mary and Martha

Call

Let us gather together and set the cares and pressures of the world aside as we seek to know God's holy presence.

Prayer

O God, as we gather together in this hour, help us have the wisdom to move beyond the cares and concerns of everyday living to hear your voice and the eternity of your holy kingdom.

Scripture

Luke 10:38-42

Hymns

"Tell Me the Stories of Jesus"
"I Love to Tell the Story"

The Christmas season, coming so near the end of the year, is often a time when companies use "functions," otherwise known as parties, to express their appreciation for all of the efforts and hard work of their employees. Such was the case for a family-owned company in the lower Midwest with operations in three different communities within a hundred mile radius. Three separate functions had to be organized and with all of the corresponding arrangements. Food had to be provided, games and entertainment worked out, and because of a commitment to all of their employees, especially those under age, special communications had to be arranged to reassure families no alcoholic beverages would be permitted on the premises. Yes, believe it or not, a company was actually planning parties to be fun without alcohol.

Although the burden of the expenses were carried by the owners, the arrangements were to be handled by the central office staff, especially one department head who had helped arrange these functions for years. One afternoon when everything was the most hectic, the department head was fretting about wanting everything to flow smoothly so everyone would have a good time. In the end, the employees at each location enjoyed getting together with their families and visiting with everyone. How like Martha the department head had been fretting over every detail and trying to keep on schedule with the planned activities, several of which did not happen because everyone was too busy having a good time visiting.

Or several years ago, there was a wonderfully bright and sensitive lady lying in her hospital bed fully aware the end was now very near. Both she and her husband of many many years had finally come to accept what now, because of disease and years, seemed inevitable. When allowed to speak and act freely, both of them had

a sense of Christian joy about them, even in the midst of her pain and suffering, which spoke volumes about the depth and reality of their faith.

But the couple was not always free to demonstrate their Christian joy. Many times visitors came, even Christians, who surprisingly enough, could not allow the couple to express their joy. Instead, these visitors came expecting the couple only to join in a premature mourning process rather than allowing the couple to openly share and celebrate in the short time which remained for the wife. Sad-faced and somber, again and again, these grieving visitors clouded up the room like a late evening summer thunderstorm.

There is such a sense of irony when scenes like this occur in hospitals, and they do occur almost every day. Those somber visitors who were coming to comfort and minister to the hospitalized lady and her husband were instead, through the deep Christian love and concern of the couple, themselves being comforted and receiving ministry. By insisting the couple must be feeling and fearing according to their own expectations, these visitors were also being like Martha who insisted the preparations for Jesus' visit must be done only her way. Mary, on the other hand, took the time to sit and truly listen to whatever thoughts Jesus had to share with her. Remember, chapter nine, verse 51, of the gospel according to Luke, clearly states Jesus was now on the way for the final time to Jerusalem. Like the woman in the hospital, Jesus knew the cross was not far away.

Or finally, there was a very fine seminary professor named George. George was a genuinely humble man who was in no way ashamed of his honest country background. George loved his family, and he loved to hunt and fish and to just be in the out-of-doors, whether that meant in the piney woods or on the open plains. In his senior years he possessed that insightful wisdom that takes the complex and somehow makes it understandable.

But George's teaching style in the seminary was a bit different. His slow Texas manner of speech combined with George's remarkable gift for couching the most profound truth within the most understandable, if not folksy, story left some of his students, who saw themselves as academic purists, leaving his room after class wondering what it was they were supposed to have taken notes on for the next test.

Through George's telling, what seemed like a simple hunting story could become a lesson on the effectiveness of parables. He could take the story of a dispute between farmers or tell a story about parenting and reflect the wisdom of Soloman. But to some of the students, this was not enough.

Again and again students would grumble and complain among themselves about George. Often they suspected he had simply become too old and was no longer able to handle the sort of academic material graduate level classes demanded. The most extreme students even considered a petition to request that George be forced to retire.

But there were students who could set aside their preconceived notions of how teaching must be and listen to George. These students found George fascinating and enlightening. For them, George was expanding their understanding of the scriptures with every class period and they could not understand the grumblers. For this group who had learned to listen, it suddenly became clear why the scriptures tell over and over again of Jesus teaching through stories and parables. Of course the grumbling and complaining students are like Martha and the students who could stop and listen to George are like Mary who listened to Jesus.

There is an important message Christians must try to hear from this passage telling us about Martha and Mary and how each responded to the presence of Jesus. Martha came before Jesus with her own preconceived agenda of what must be done for things to be right. Mary came before the Lord prepared to set everything else aside and to listen.

In so many ways and through so many situations in life, the Lord may well be trying to speak to us or to use us. If we approach these as Martha did, with our own fixed ideas of what must be done for things to be "right," we are very likely going to miss out on some wonderful blessings. If, however, we can set aside our fixed ideas and listen, as Mary did, the Lord may well be able to teach us many very special and beautiful lessons about life.

As is so often the case when we encounter the scriptures, we are challenged to make some choices. Our passage today asks each one of us to examine our own lives and see whether we have been closed or open in our spirit as we have come before the Lord. Then our passage challenges each one of us to make a personal commitment to being open to allowing the Lord to help us be more as God would want us to be.

Dear Lord, so often we approach the situations which confront us in life with our own notions of how they must be worked out rather than seeking your leadership in guiding us to your solutions. Open our hearts, Lord, so we might hear your words of guidance and wisdom. Through Christ we pray. Amen.

One Day at a Time

Call

Come let us worship together all who would live this day to serve the Lord.

Prayer

O God, as we gather today, help us see the ways you have demonstrated your love for us. Help us to know and believe you are with us and sustaining us in all that we do to serve you. In Christ we pray. Amen.

Scripture

Matthew 6:19-34

Hymns

"Seek Ye First"
"More Love to Thee, O Christ"

Most likely, very few of us will have any significant long-term advance notice of what will eventually be our cause of death. At twenty-nine, Bill, who had labored long and hard to work his way up from his humble beginnings, was hearing his doctor explain the almost always fatal form of cancer the exhaustive tests were now indicating was present in Bill's body.

Cancer! How could this be happening to Bill? Only months before, his third child, a son, was born, and now this. The questions were overwhelming. Could the cancer be stopped? If not, how long would Bill have? Who would be there for the children? Would the little boy just born ever get to know his father?

There were answers of a sort for some of the questions. The doctor went on to explain how patients with this form of cancer had a very slim survival rate and more often than not the patient had only a brief amount of time remaining. But, if Bill could stand the treatment, the doctor said some radiation therapy combined with an intensive level of an experimental chemotherapy could very well buy Bill and his family some time. The doctor, however, was not offering any guarantees but told Bill the question was no longer what was going to be his cause of death, but when.

Bill's faith had always been very important to him, but in the face of this kind of news, everything seemed out of control for a while. As if the news of the cancer were not bad enough, as Bill and his family studied all of the information they could find about the particular cancer Bill had, they discovered the quality of life he could expect to "enjoy" was anything but encouraging. Much more often than not, the marriages of cancer patients fail to survive the stress of a prolonged battle to stop the disease. Often the physical condition of patients is markedly reduced, along with their overall general health. Some of the side effects from the radiation and chemotherapy are often long term if not permanent. In general, this would be a rough battle even under the best conditions.

But Bill had an overwhelming love for his family and he so desperately wanted to see and guide his children, even the newborn son, through to adulthood. In his heart of hearts, from the depth of his soul, Bill asked God for just one gift: to please allow him to see his youngest child grow up.

And so the battle lines were drawn and what became a series of severe treatments began. Intense radiation made Bill very ill, and later the chemotherapy would do its share to add to the misery. As time passed, it became clear to friends and family alike how critical Bill's condition really was.

Finally some good news came. The first round of the battle went to Bill as the cancer was sent into remission. Everyone's first thoughts and prayers were of thanksgiving for Bill having been given more time. Yet, in the unspoken background, like the backdrop to a stage play, was the clear understanding "remission" does not have the same meaning as "cure" and there were more battles to come in this war.

Bill very much enjoyed the times when the cancer was in remission. He was able to return to his job and even to enjoy a near normal level of general activity. His family, his church, his community, and his job, all received the very best Bill knew how to give. But the remission did not last forever.

Once again the cancer returned and the severe treatments had to be resumed. Again the treatments worked and the cancer was in remission. This cycle of recurrence, treatment, and remission would repeat itself several times bringing Bill very near to death more than once over the years.

When one visited with Bill, especially if he was in remission, you sensed he possessed a clarity of values one seldom runs across in a man as young as Bill. It was rare when Bill was asked how he could possibly cope with staring death in the face again and again if he did not respond with his favorite answer, "You just have to take life one day at a time." You simply could not be around Bill for very long without knowing beyond a shadow of a doubt how much this man loved and trusted the Lord for even the simple things in life.

Isn't it strange how Bill, who from the time he was twenty-nine had battled cancer every day of his life, could so clearly understand the words of Jesus calling us to live life one day at a time? Bill had an absolute faith in Christ that would not be swayed or shaken no matter what the circumstances, including his own life-threatening and very debilitating rounds with cancer. Why then do so many of us who are relatively healthy tend to have such problems with fretting about yesterday or worrying about tomorrow? Barring the unexpected, we have considerably more time the Lord can use us to work out whatever situation we are confronting.

By the way, Bill's one request was granted. Twenty years after he first heard the report from his doctor about cancer, the disease would no longer be put into remission. Twenty years after their baby boy was born Bill would die. This was twenty years that Bill demonstrated not only how to live life one day at a time, but how to live it with dignity and be a contributing member of the community along the way. During the periods of remission Bill earned his way into management where he worked, served actively within his church, and was even elected to public office several times over the years. Maybe to Bill, however, one of the most wonderful events of all happened in the spring just before he died. In that last spring Bill got to see his baby boy graduate from college and he knew the blessing of seeing all three children grow up. How did Bill not only manage to survive the agony of two decades of intensive therapy but go on to personally celebrate and make the most of the periods of remission with which he was blessed? Bill took the words of Jesus, his Lord, very seriously and lived life as the Lord said it is to be lived, by holding true to his faith and doing the very best he could, one day at a time.

Prayer

Dear Lord, forgive us when we have been slow to keep our focus on the day with which you have blessed us. Give us the wisdom to learn from our yesterdays and plan wisely for our tomorrows, but to live our lives to the very best of our abilities today. Through Christ our Lord we pray. Amen.

What About Jonah?

Call

Come, let all who would seek to follow the will of the Lord gather this day and worship.

Prayer

Dear Lord, as we gather this day, touch our hearts with an assurance you are our good shepherd, ever present to guide and care for us, even when we have turned our hearts to seeking our own ways. In Christ we pray. Amen.

Scripture

Jonah, chapter 1

Hymns

"God Will Take Care of You"
"Because He Lives"

Few would argue the world we live in is a rapidly changing place. The advances in technology have come so quickly we hardly have time to become adjusted to one new development before another is introduced. New forms of computer technology are introduced before the older forms are fully learned. New technologies are coming so quickly one can hardly depend on today's equipment being compatible or even usable in tomorrow's market. There are some who do not know why we say we "dial a phone number" because they have never seen a rotary dial on a telephone. We have some younger people who cannot tell time from the round face of an analogue clock and have no clue how such chronological terms as "half past" or "a quarter till" came to exist in our current world of digital timepieces.

Doubt is a normal part of almost every phase of life itself. Huge "blue chip" corporations, once considered to be the rock solid backbone of the world economy, have in some cases completely disappeared from the economic scene and in other cases are struggling for all they are worth to remain competitive in today's business world.

Even jobs once thought to be permanent and secure for generation after generation are now subject to change. Some types of work, once done by members of the same family for over a hundred years, today are being replaced by advanced machines. Some jobs are relocating to different parts of the country or even to different countries. Other jobs are changing technically so much they hardly resemble the occupations they once represented.

Is there any wonder then, with our culture in such a period of doubt and uncertainty, how some who are seeking to be true to their Christian walk become worried and fearful they may somehow mistake God's intention for their lives or in some way inadvertently drift astray and miss some special ministry God would have had them be about in the world? It is to this fear the book of Jonah offers a wonderful word of assurance.

Jonah is certainly another of those colorful people the Lord was able to use in carrying God's message to the world. One can hardly consider Jonah as an average evangelist. Jonah did, however, hold a deep personal faith in God and as contrary and stubborn as he might have been, in the hands of the Lord, Jonah became an evangelist and a prophet.

Our passage today opens with God calling Jonah to arise and go to Nineveh where God intends for Jonah to deliver a call for repentance to the people there. Jonah clearly has no intention of going to Nineveh and instead heads in the opposite direction by boarding a ship at Joppa headed for Tarshish.

With the ship now en route, Jonah assumes he has escaped God's call. God, seeing Jonah's efforts to flee, surrounds the ship with a storm and soon everyone learns Jonah is the cause. Jonah tells the seamen to throw him overboard whereupon God sends a big fish or a whale to swallow Jonah and take him back to dry land. Once Jonah arrives back on dry land, God again calls him to go to Nineveh and this time Jonah carries out the mission.

It is at this point in the story of Jonah where Christians should begin to see a real security blanket for believers. Is it possible Jonah's story is so familiar the obvious tends to get overlooked? For generations Christians have argued about whether the story is true or a teaching parable. Could a human have been swallowed by a big fish or a whale and survived the experience for three days?

Some even question if the revival generated by Jonah's delivery of God's message ever occurred at all and if it did, why were there no historical records of it?

For Christians of our day, however, the heart of the message clearly recommends a concept of security we may have never recognized before. Throughout Jonah's experience, the question stands as to who will ultimately be in control of the destiny of Jonah, a true believer. God will, of course!

It is God who calls Jonah to service. Jonah refuses and runs the other way. God then demonstrates how all of the resources of the universe are under God's command in providing the guidance for one who truly believes. God does not hesitate to use a storm that threatens all aboard the ship but never causes the others any harm. Once Jonah has been thrown overboard, God uses a great fish or a whale to swallow Jonah and transport him back to dry land where Jonah can resume his journey to Nineveh.

Jonah's relationship with God seems quite close. God talks to Jonah, and Jonah appears very accustomed to and comfortable with talking to God. It is not that Jonah does not love God but rather that Jonah simply does not like the Ninevites and does not want to share God's word with them. But God never gives up on Jonah and is willing to use whatever resources are required to guide Jonah into the mission God has planned for him.

And the same is true today for all Christians who know and love the Lord. Be very assured God still has big fish to use to bring us back to dry land if necessary. God can still send the storms to bring us to our senses if we will listen in no other way. Even if we were to act like spoiled children, as did Jonah, God is more than capable of managing the situation. We are indeed secure in the hands of "a loving and compassionate God" as Jonah puts it.

There is one other thought which springs forth from this passage. As children of God, we might want to be very careful who we choose to hate. As Jonah discovered, it may well be those very people to whom God would have us deliver the good news of God's redeeming love through Christ. And remember, God still has plenty of storms and big fish to help us get the message there.

Prayer

O God, thank you for being so loving and understanding that you will use whatever it takes to help us know where you would have us serve. Through Christ our Lord we pray. Amen.

Prayer

Call

Let us gather together for worship, all who would come before the Lord in song and prayer.

Prayer

Dear Lord, we often exclude your leadership from the areas of life we deem secular. Help us to open our hearts to hearing how you would be involved with all that we are and not just a portion when we are in trouble. Through Christ we pray. Amen.

Scripture

James 3:13-18

Hymns

"Sweet Hour of Prayer"
"Every Time I Feel the Spirit"

It was a cold and wintry evening as the prayer group gathered and waited for the pastor to arrive. Obviously something had delayed the pastor, and when she finally came it was apparent to everyone all was not well. Then came the announcement one of the church members had died earlier that afternoon.

Only a little over a week before, the church member had quietly entered the hospital to undergo elective surgery to correct what might best be called a cosmetic problem. At the prayer meeting a week ago the group had been told of a serious problem that came up during the surgery leaving the church member in an unstable condition. The hospitalized church member was then placed on the prayer list specifically asking God to provide the healing necessary to restore her to health and return her to the fellowship of the church.

But the prayer requests through the past week had not been honored. The church member died, and the questions in the minds of the prayer group members on that bitterly cold evening were many. Like many prayer groups, this group kept a record of their prayer requests and made note of the answers to their

prayers, as they recognized them, and the group had begun to develop a confidence in the power of prayer. But this time the church member for whom they prayed had died.

Finally one among the prayer group that evening asked the pastor how this could have happened. Everyone in the prayer group knew it was God's desire to heal the sick and the brokenhearted, so why were their prayers not answered?

With the winter wind whistling around the corners of the church building, the pastor, with a loving and contrite heart, asked how many in the prayer group, before last week's surgery, had been praying for the church member especially in light of the cosmetic problem about which everyone knew she was very self-conscious. Not one person, including the pastor, had been praying for her. The pastor went on to explain there are some questions to which answers will be given only in heaven, but it seemed clear at this point that their Christian fellowship had failed to be about caring and praying for a very precious member when the church certainly knew of the member's need. There is a time when even the church must accept the results of its choices and had the prayer group been lifting this person in prayer when the group first became aware of the area of self-consciousness, events might have gone a different direction.

Some years later, in a completely different part of the country, another scene was being played out which profoundly describes the way prayer is often viewed today. The car wreck had been especially violent. The state police speculated from the evidence at the scene a mechanical failure in the eastbound car somehow caused it to veer into the median where it began tumbling end over end into the westbound lane where it hit the car of a college student on the way home for midsemester break. Both drivers were transported to a nearby major hospital where each was received by trauma teams and both were quickly rushed into extensive surgery.

By the time the first surgical team came out to report to the relatives, the family of each driver had arrived at the hospital, and as can sometimes happen in a crisis of this magnitude, the two families had somehow met and were comforting each other. The surgeons reported the student was in critical condition and what developed in the next twenty-four hours would determine what sort of recovery could be expected.

A short while later, the team of surgeons who had worked on the eastbound driver came out to report. Again the patient was listed in critical condition and the next twenty-four hours would determine what sort of recovery could be expected, but this time the doctor added, "All we can do now is pray."

"All we can do now is pray." How many times is that thought expressed in what are presumed to be hopeless or rather humanly helpless situations? But is this really what prayer is all about? The phrase "all we can do now" seems to suggest prayer can be considered an action of last resort when all other human efforts have been exhausted. This approach to prayer seems to be the logical final step to "God helps those who help themselves." Do all we humanly can do and then turn to God for that which we cannot manage ourselves.

What many people do not realize, however, is this good old saying, "God helps those who help themselves" is not even remotely close to any biblical teaching. Over and over again we read in the scriptures of how God stands with and provides for those who wait upon the Lord and who seek God's guidance in every step through life. We also read in the scriptures of those, like David, who struck out doing their own works and we can hear the agony David expresses so eloquently in the Psalms for his sins.

Fortunately God is loving and merciful, and even when we are not always the loving children we might be, our prayers are answered. Miraculously, both drivers experienced near complete recoveries and both families, who spent weeks in the hospital together, became good friends.

Those who love God have been given absolute and total free access to come before the creator and sustainer of the entire universe at any time, from any place, and under any circumstances within which we may find ourselves. We are encouraged to pray about every burden we might have in our own lives, and we are encouraged to be sensitive to the concerns of those around us and lift the needs of others before the Lord in prayer as well.

In the gift of prayer the Lord has offered us not a tool but a relationship. Prayer is not something we do when we need something from God, but it is the certainty we may walk and talk with the Lord through our everyday experiences just as surely as did Adam and Eve in the Garden of Eden. Prayer is the promise of God's presence and attention in every moment of life like the very best friend we have ever had. To Christians, prayer is not just something they are expected to do; prayer becomes a part of who Christians are, friends with the living God.

As we hear our scripture today calling us to be about praying for each other, do we hear God's call to living a life of friendship and caring? A life open to caring and being sensitive to and accepting of those around us, for how else could we possibly know their needs well enough to be about lifting those needs to the Lord in prayer? A life based on a total trust in the Lord, for how else would we be free to share everything without reservation in prayer? Or are we still thinking of prayer only as something we are called to do?

Prayer

Dear Lord, thank you for loving us so much you would hear every thought we would share with you. Through Christ our Lord we pray. Amen.

The Name of God

Call

Come! Let all who would stand firm for the cause of Christ join together this day to celebrate in worship and song.

Prayer

O God, you have been so patient with all of those whom you have called through the ages. With Moses and the Hebrew children, with the prophets and tribes in captivity, with the early church and with us today, and yet you call us to righteousness. Help us to know and proclaim for all to hear and understand: you are called love. In Christ we pray. Amen.

Scripture

Exodus 3:13-15

Hymns

"God of Many Names"
"Immortal, Invisible, God Only Wise"

For one reason or another, people have probably always placed a tremendous importance in knowing a person's name. This is certainly true in today's world. The casual mention of being familiar with a high profile personality is often calculated to generate admiration, respect, and curiosity. The mention of having been sent by a person of rank brings with it authority. Being privileged to use a person's private nickname can develop closeness and bonding. We still use names as an integral part of our personal communications.

Who among us has not known nicknames of endearment shared only by family and friends? Or names given to each other by members of the same athletic team or people in the same club? Such names all carry special meanings and must be carefully chosen. Nicknames have the power to convey deep levels of love and acceptance when used properly as well as to inflict great personal pain and suffering when used maliciously.

Names often clearly suggest authority. Who has never been in or known of a situation where authority has not been recognized? County election commissioners are not always widely publicized positions. One election day a commissioner stopped by to see how things were going at one of the election polling places. Almost all of the election judges operating the poll knew the commissioner. One new judge, however, appointed from the opposing party, had never met the commissioner. The new judge, without seeking to learn who the commissioner was and seeing the commissioner was in a restricted area visiting with several of the other judges, came up and rudely ordered the commissioner to move back into a public area. The commissioner smiled pleasantly, unruffled by the circumstances, and asked, "Do you know who I am?"

Moses, now eighty years old and having lived in the desert for the past forty years, has again heard the voice of God calling him to lead the Hebrew children out of Egyptian bondage. This is the same Moses who had heard God's call to lead the Hebrew children out of Egypt forty years earlier and who had taken matters into his own hands only to end up fleeing for his life to the desert. It seems reasonable Moses would want to know exactly who is now giving him his marching orders to go back to Egypt to try again to lead God's children out of bondage.

In Exodus 3:14, God gives Moses the name YHWH, often translated in the scriptures as "I AM WHO I AM." It is the great "I AM" who will lead the Hebrew children out of bondage into a new life. Moses is to tell the children of Israel YHWH, the God who knew and loved

Abraham, Isaac, and Jacob, has sent him, Moses, to lead them out of Egypt.

In the past few generations, a great deal of study and effort have been devoted to understanding the full meaning of the name God gave to Moses. YHWH appears to be a form of the verb "to be" and can, depending on one's choice of the form it represents, develop several powerful images of the nature of God. Most interpretations suggest the nature of God is transcendent, not to be dependent upon or altered by any circumstances or conditions the human mind could imagine.

There seems however, to be an irony at work in such theological scholarship seeking to discover the nature of God through independent research into the divine name given to Moses. With no intent to be critical, let us try to do the following as clearly and concisely as possible: "Describe a delta xenon hypothermal transducing photo integrator." If we are having a bit of trouble even getting started with a description it is because no such piece of equipment has yet been invented.

By the same principle, were you to have asked Moses to describe as clearly and concisely as possible a device called a "television," Moses would surely have been as confused as we were a moment ago. Most of us today, however, can describe a television. Why? Because televisions have now been invented and the characteristics they possess are very familiar to most of us.

The point of course is with the birth of Jesus, we have been given a firsthand view of God in the clearest expression of human terms possible. Jesus even told us directly how all who have seen him have seen God, for he and God are one. In Jesus we have a standard by which, when we are in doubt, we may compare the true nature of God.

So is the transcendent quality implied in the divine name given to Moses consistent with the nature and personality the scriptures record for us about Jesus? One could reasonably say that it is. Although Jesus was of this world, he also would not be swayed by the world away from the task for which he was born. When confronted by what must have been Satan's most alluring and beguiling temptations in the wilderness, Jesus would not be swayed. And even when confronted by the power of the mighty Roman Empire and faced with the brutality and humiliation of death on a cross, Jesus would not be swayed. Surely it would be safe to say Jesus was a clear personification of the "I AM WHO I AM." And just as surely it is the same voice that called Moses to lead the children of Israel out of bondage that through the life and words of Jesus, leads us out of bondage today.

Just as Moses would proclaim for all the world how God had led the Hebrew children out of the hopeless depths of slavery in Egypt into freedom and eventually the promised land, let us each one be about the task of proclaiming it is the Christ who would lead the hopeless out of the various forms of human slavery that would hold us captive in the world today.

Prayer

O Lord, help us realize all of the times you have reached into human history and led us out of the grasp of human bondage. Celebrate through us, O God, that in your kingdom there are no powers great enough to enslave the hearts of your children. Through Christ our Lord we pray. Amen.

Counting the Cost

Call

Let us gather and worship in the holy name of Christ all who would commit their lives to serving the risen Lord.

Prayer

Dear Lord, help us today to realize the cost of the commitment to follow and to serve you. Help us choose with a knowing heart, for eternity rests in the balance. In Christ we pray. Amen.

Scripture

Luke 14:25-35

Hymns

"Are Ye Able"
"Jesu, Jesu"

The air was charged with excitement as Diego came forward on the cool March evening to be baptized. Diego was twenty-two years old, but he felt like a child as the tears of joy streamed down his face. The only cloud hanging over the otherwise joyful service of celebration was that his parents had refused to come and witness Diego's baptism. The church Diego had chosen to join was not of the same Christian tradition as his family's background and thus at the last minute his parents elected not to come.

Weeks of serious discussion regarding the possible costs and repercussions had gone into Diego's decision to join this particular church. Diego was aware his parents might respond as strongly and negatively as they did, but considering how much Diego knew his parents loved him he had hoped they would accept his decision without a serious protest. As it turned out, they would not.

Diego had dropped out of college and was seriously underemployed even though he was working over fifty hours a week between two part-time jobs. His parents had been letting him use one of their cars until he could work something out, but now they told him he could use it to go to work and to church only once a week. Diego could not use their car to go to church on Sunday evening or on Wednesday.

With little room to bargain, Diego accepted their wishes and quietly but proudly began walking the eight miles to church when he could not drive. Diego was proud of his family, and although he could not understand their behavior at the moment, he did not wish for anyone to know how they had restricted his use of their car. One evening a church member very diplomatically questioned Diego about his means of transportation and made arrangements to see to it Diego would not have to walk again.

As the next few weeks passed, tensions between Diego and his parents grew worse. During a visit with the pastor, Diego admitted he did not realize his decision to follow Christ was going to take his family away from him. Diego then smiled and explained that for the time being, the church was his family.

Later that spring Diego would feel God's call to return to college and to enter full-time Christian ministry. When Diego's parents heard he was returning to college, they were very pleased. When Diego told them he felt called to enter full-time Christian ministry, they were considerably less happy.

The summer came and Diego worked and saved all he could planning to reenter college. Nothing seemed to be working out for him. During the preceding winter Diego had had two automobile accidents on the icy streets. Repairing cars had seriously depleted what little savings Diego had. The rest of his savings Diego had loaned to his parents and he dreaded the confrontation it would take to ask for the money to be returned.

Finally one day Diego summoned up the nerve to bring up the subject. Diego was very surprised at how calm and reassured he felt when the explosion finally occurred. Deep in his soul, Diego could hear the Lord reminding him to love his father, no matter how upset his father became. Diego tried to do just as the Lord was telling him to do. Finally Diego felt as if the Lord was leading him to bring an end to this situation by giving his father the borrowed money. Diego waited his turn to speak and softly explained to his father how he loved him much more than the money and Diego was making his father a gift of the money. Diego's father owed him nothing. To Diego's surprise his father became even more angry than before, and their relationship became so strained they could hardly be around each other without a confrontation.

About midsummer Diego finally received some good news. He had been accepted into a Christian college several hundred miles away. Now it seemed urgent for Diego to find some sort of automobile to use to go to school. Two weeks before Diego was due to leave, his fraternal aunt called and wondered if Diego would be interested in his late grandfather's car. Excited and feeling as if the Lord was finally beginning to bring things together for him, Diego told his aunt he certainly was interested and arrangements were made to meet at the state license office to make the title transfer.

Diego's heart was pounding as he met his aunt at the state office. When their turn came at the clerk's window, the aunt explained what they were trying to do and brought out the title. The clerk pointed out the grandfather's signature needed to be on the title to transfer it and Diego's aunt stated that was no problem as she signed the grandfather's name. The clerk now demanded a death certificate which the aunt did not have with her.

Everyone went back to the aunt's home to dig through the family papers for the death certificate, but it was not to be found. The aunt said she would find it

and meet Diego again at the state office to complete the transfer the next day.

That night in his prayer time Diego impatiently asked God why the transfer had not taken place. In a voice as clear as if someone had said it standing right next to him, Diego heard the Lord tell him, "Ask your father." It was about two in the morning and Diego was not about to create an incident by waking his father at that hour. Again Diego returned to prayer and again the Lord told him to "Ask your father." Diego refused and a third time he heard the same message.

Slowly and cautiously Diego eased the door of his father's room open and whispered softly, "Dad?" To his surprise his father was awake and knew exactly what Diego wanted. He told Diego to get some sleep and he would explain what was going on in the morning.

Morning came and Diego's father explained. Diego would have to pay inheritance tax if he accepted his grandfather's car. The tax would have been almost all Diego had left in savings.

But the Lord had been doing something far more important than protecting Diego from the tax on the car. That night the Lord had honored Diego's commitment to Christ—a commitment so real Diego had been willing to give up the most precious possession he had, his family. In having Diego seek his father's advice in the middle of the night, the Lord restored the very close relationship Diego had always treasured with his family.

Years later when Diego was asked if he would have kept his commitment to the Lord even if his family had not been returned to him, Diego's answer was, "There was no other choice."

Today we must remember when we take up our cross and commit to wearing the name Christian, that which we treasure most must go into our commitment as well. There is always a cost for those who would choose to follow Christ, and the commitment is all or nothing before the Lord. When the tough times come and we must choose between the world and the Lord, would that we all could join Diego in saying there is no other choice but to follow Christ.

Prayer

Dear Lord, give us the courage to pay the price of commitment. The rewards of faith are for an eternity. In Christ we pray. Amen.

Reaching for Eternity

Call

Let all who would walk with the Lord now and in eternity gather this day to lift the joy in your soul in worship and praise.

Prayer

Dear Lord, as we gather together today, help us to know your presence and your love, and help us to reach to commit more and more of our life to walking with you. In Christ we pray. Amen.

Scripture

John 3:16-18

Hymns

"The Voice of God Is Calling"
"What Does the Lord Require"

Ronnie had worked as a roofer since his junior year in high school. Every spring as the weather warmed up and the days became hotter, Ronnie was always one of the very first to shed his shirt and get as deep a suntan as he could possibly get. When school started for his senior year, his classmates, especially the young ladies, were impressed with his strong lean muscles and his deep dark suntan. Ronnie, never having been outstanding as a student before, enjoyed the attention for a change.

Now Ronnie was twenty-five and his crew was working on a strange sort of house for that part of the country. The house had a very high and almost flat section in the roof, nearly four full stories above the ground. There was certainly nothing difficult about getting the roofing laid on the flat section; it was just in a hard to reach location.

Ronnie, being the crew foreman and the most experienced member of the crew, climbed up to take a look at exactly what would be involved in getting the materials up to that level. Just as Ronnie walked over to the edge of the roof to call down to the crew below the unthinkable happened. A nail in the decking caught the edge of Ronnie's shoe throwing him off balance and Ronnie hurled over the edge toward the ground headfirst.

For what seemed like an eternity everyone stood helplessly watching as Ronnie fell. In what seemed like a miracle, Ronnie, very shaken and a bit bewildered, had landed in a huge sandpile the trucks had delivered a few days earlier to be used by the bricklayers. Ronnie was taken to the hospital just as a precaution, but he walked over to the friend's car who drove him there. Everyone breathed a sigh of relief as they saw Ronnie headed to the hospital, and the fall was the topic of conversation for the rest of the day.

For Ronnie, however, everything was not quite that simple. As he rode to the hospital, his mind began to clear and Ronnie began to remember his thoughts as he was falling. Ronnie's body now hurting all over, he remembered thinking, "I'm going to die and, Lord, I am not ready." That was all he had thought. He was going to die. This was the first time Ronnie had ever even considered the day would come when he would die. Now Ronnie had stared death in the face and as he realized what had happened, he began to shake all over.

When they reached the emergency room at the hospital, everything went very routinely. Many papers had to be filled out, but Ronnie's boss had met them at the hospital and he helped out with these matters. Ronnie was not feeling well and the nurses quickly took him to an examining room so he could lie down.

While the doctors in the emergency room ran several tests, Ronnie's boss contacted Ronnie's wife Beth to let her know of the fall and that he was pretty sure Ronnie would be all right. Beth left work and rushed to the hospital.

The test results were not totally clear. The doctors, astounded at how well Ronnie was doing after a four-story fall, explained that although everything seemed OK, one test came back with a borderline result. They recommended Ronnie stay in the hospital overnight for observation until they could be sure. The doctors tried to reassure Ronnie and Beth that they were almost positive Ronnie was going to be as good as new. It was just better to be safe and have Ronnie there at the hospital in the unlikely event something should develop. Because of the special nature of the one borderline test and because as the working day was ending the ER waiting area was already overflowing with Ronnie's friends and coworkers wanting to visit, the doctors made the decision to admit Ronnie to the Intensive Care Unit with visiting privileges restricted to his immediate family until nine o'clock when Ronnie would begin a watched time of rest until morning.

Originally Ronnie was upset with the decision to isolate him, but as nine o'clock came, he was so uncomfortable he really did not mind no longer having to visit even with his wife. But the whole hospital experience was totally new to Ronnie. The closest he had ever come to being in the hospital was the two times Beth had been in to give birth to their two children.

The sights, sounds, and smells of the hospital gave Ronnie a lot to think about. Somewhere out of sight, a person would groan now and then, and it sounded to Ronnie like a serious groan. Soon the lights were dimmed and the cubical doors were closed and apart from the sounds of the monitors attached to him, Ronnie had little to listen to but his own thoughts.

Deep down, something told Ronnie he was going to be fine. But the thoughts during the fall kept coming back to Ronnie. Death was at hand, and he knew he was not ready. But what did he need to do to be ready?

About midnight, Ronnie asked the nurse checking on him if there was a chaplain on duty and if there was a possibility the chaplain could come in and visit with him. The nurse said she would check. In about ten minutes the chaplain politely pushed open the door and asked if he could come in. Ronnie smiled and nodded okay. For the next twenty minutes Ronnie shared with the chaplain everything that had led to his being in the ICU. Then as Ronnie came to feel he could trust the chaplain, he shared the thoughts that had flashed through his mind during the fall.

Ronnie looked straight at the chaplain and told him he had never gone to church or Sunday school much. In fact he only knew one verse from the Bible, one Ronnie had learned when he was just a little boy. The chaplain smiled and asked Ronnie which verse it was. "God so loved the world that he gave his only begotten son that whoever believes in him should not die, but have eternal life." Ronnie bowed his head for a moment without a word and then looked back at the chaplain and said, "Chaplain, those words did not make a lick of sense to me as a kid. I memorized them so I'd get a star from the Sunday school teacher. Today I could have died, and I know it. Now those words mean something to me. Do you think it's too late tonight for us to talk about it?"

Prayer

Dear Lord, we thank you that you so often have given us second chances— that you love us so much you will nurture us through even the worst of circumstances without giving up on us—that your love stands with us even when we face death. In Christ we pray. Amen.

The Paradox

Call

Come, let us enter the house of the Lord with praise and song in our hearts, for life eternal belongs to those who would give their lives to the Lord.

Prayer

O God, as we come together today, draw us ever closer to being the people you would have us to be. Take our lives and mold and shape them bringing them ever closer to your life, O Christ. We give you all that we are, Lord. In Christ we pray. Amen.

Scripture

Matthew 16:24-28

"Take Up Thy Cross"
"Stand Up, Stand Up for Jesus"

It had been almost a year now since Chris had been made vice president in charge of production. As he sat behind the large executive desk and looked around the mahogany paneled office, Chris was thinking to himself, "What have I done?"

Chris had been with the company almost twenty-five years. He started as a helper running errands for the people who operated the big machines. It was almost too good to be true the way everyone noticed Chris' hard work and positive attitude. Before he knew it, Chris had been promoted to being a machine operator, and he immediately began to set new production records.

For ten years he ran the big machines and was considered the very best operator in the company. When new higher volume machines were purchased, Chris set even higher production records for everyone to try to catch. But no one ever did.

It was when he had been with the company a little over ten years that Chris was made an assistant foreman. There were no arguments from any of the crew that Chris had earned the promotion. Chris worked with the operators showing them all of the little things he had figured out which helped him set the records. His help paid off as the average overall production increased by 6 percent when operating at peak rate.

Chris' record continued to be very impressive and now he was receiving attention from the right people in the front office. Chris was noticing how he was getting special projects from the front office to accomplish along with his regular job duties, while the other assistant foremen were never given such assignments.

It would be another five years before Chris received his next promotion. When the foreman retired, Chris was promoted to full foreman. Again, Chris being chosen to become foreman was hardly a surprise to anyone.

As foreman, Chris was beginning to grow uncomfortable with some of the things he was hearing in and around the executive management meetings he was now required to attend. There were parties planned and activities considered that Chris never felt should be a part of the way a company does business. Chris figured, however, he would remain silent since he was not directly involved and he really needed to keep his job. Whenever he could do it, Chris stayed on the floor with the production crews where he knew he was among friends.

Two years after Chris became foreman, tragedy opened the door for another promotion. The plant superintendent was killed on New Year's Eve in an automobile accident while on the way home from the company party. Chris was a bit reluctant to accept this new promotion. When Chris did not give his reply immediately, an acquaintance from the president's staff just happened to drop by to congratulate Chris and in the conversation mentioned how in the corporate world things tend to be "up or out." Chris became the plant superintendent.

As the plant superintendent, life for Chris and his family became more comfortable than they ever imagined it could be. Chris now received a very nice company car, a full membership in the country club, an enhanced stock option plan, and other assorted perks. Chris' salary also jumped enough that his wife immediately proposed they should build a new house over in the area where the other company executives lived. Reluctantly, Chris gave in and agreed to building the new house.

Now the executive functions were mandatory for Chris. Chris' wife loved to attend the various get-togethers when the spouses were included. But Chris never told her about the times when the spouses were not included. At first Chris was something of a wallflower at the functions. Chris tried to meet and talk with the clients, but for the most part they seemed bored talking about business. They were there to relax and unwind, not to hammer out deals and discuss production schedules.

One afternoon the president of the company called Chris for a visit. Their visit was very friendly and they talked about family, production matters, and who had had the best round of golf lately. Then the conversation turned to Chris' lack of enthusiasm at the business functions. The message was ever so subtle but very very clear. Chris understood he must either "get with the program or look for another job." Chris agreed he would try harder.

Chris did try harder. At the very next function he had a little more to drink than he should have and ended up spending the night with one of their female clients. Now what would he do? How could he face his family? The company people told him not to worry

about it; they would cover for him. This sort of thing just happens. But this sort of thing was not acceptable to Chris.

Chris struggled constantly with the guilt of what he had done. More functions came and went and he would not make that mistake again, but now he was noticing others were involved with providing all sorts of entertainment to help their clients relax. Chris made very sure he remained in control of his own behavior, but the sick feeling would not go away.

Finally one day the really big news came. Chris was called into the president's office again. This time several of the major stockholders were there, and they informed Chris he had been selected to become the new vice president of production. Chris tried to look enthused as he smiled and shook hands with everyone in the room.

But now Chris was sitting in his vice president's office wondering. Chris had everything he had ever dreamed of having, so why was he feeling so empty? Ever since Chris had learned of becoming a vice president a single Bible passage kept popping into his mind again and again. "What does it profit a person to gain the whole world if he forfeits his soul?" Chris finally bowed his head and whispered, "Dear God, is it too late?"

Prayer

Dear Lord, so many times we find ourselves having gone in ways we know you would not have had us go. Give us the courage, Lord, to come home. Through Christ our Lord we pray. Amen.

Hard Times

Call

Let all who are weary and wounded and who would celebrate the love and forgiveness of our Lord Jesus Christ gather this day for worship.

Prayer

O God, we would so like to ask that you pave the road of our lives with only comforts and pleasures, yet in our hearts we know these would not help us grow and mature. Give us the wisdom to see your presence in even the adversities of life, Lord. In Christ we pray. Amen.

Scripture

Romans 5:1-11

Hymns

"It Is Good to Sing Thy Praises"
"I Know Whom I Have Believed"

Jay's first year of being a seminary student had not been a great deal of fun. Between working more hours than he was recommended to and the long hours of study a full-time graduate student must put in, there had been little to celebrate. But now it was summer and at least for a while the study was out of the way.

One hot sultry Friday evening in July, Jay allowed himself the entertainment of looking at used cars. Before long Jay was sitting behind the wheel of a new top-of-the-line car with air-conditioning that worked. In that instant, as Jay sat comfortably relaxing in some of the most wonderful car seats he had ever been in, the entertainment began turning into trouble.

The skillful salesman had Jay take the car for a ride. The sleek powerful four-door pulled away from stoplights with the ease of a sports car. The car stereo had a sound quality like Jay had only heard from home systems he had dreamed one day he might be able to afford. As Jay switched from station to station to hear how each different type of music sounded, the salesman was beginning to hear the sound of a sale.

That night Jay passed up the car and for a week he watched every day as he passed by the lot to see if the beautiful gray car was still there. Jay wondered, first, if such a car were really necessary for a pastor and, second, if it fit into the budget of a seminary student. Finally Jay got around to asking God if he should go ahead on faith and buy what seemed like his dream car.

For almost a week Jay prayed about whether to buy the car or not, but he never seemed to hear a clear answer from the Lord. One voice seemed to be saying, "What you do is up to you" while another seemed to be telling him, "Do you really think you need a car like that?" Jay agonized as he sought the leadership of the Lord about the car. He wanted to believe the first voice, but the second was asking the question Jay did not want to answer. Of course Jay did not need a car like this one. But it would be a good investment, and this type of car was built better than the lesser models on the market.

Even as the Lord brought many signs and people to suggest Jay was rationalizing his desire to buy the big car, Jay could hear none of them. Even on the day Jay finally decided to sign the deal and get the gray car, God seemed to be telling him this was not the thing to do. Jay rationalized it was his own fiscally conservative upbringing speaking since no one in Jay's immediate family had ever owned a car like this one. So Jay signed the papers for the car.

That next weekend Jay took a trip in the new car. It was only a couple of hundred miles each way, but it was a lesson in the economics of automobile transportation. Jay had been used to the economy of a small six-cylinder engine. The powerful V-8 in the new car performed very nicely; however, it could hardly pass a gas station without needing to be filled up. Then Jay noticed his dream car was using about a quart of oil every few hundred miles. At this rate, the fuel for the gray car was going to cost more than the car payment. Within forty eight hours, Jay was wishing he had not gotten the car.

When Jay went back to the dealer, he got his second major lesson from the new car. The warm and friendly salesman who had sold him the car no longer existed. Oh, the same person was there at the dealership, but the same personality was gone and in its place was a cold matter of fact personality who had no difficulty at all in telling Jay the car was Jay's own problem now and there was nothing the dealership could do to help him. When Jay mentioned the oil the car was using, the salesman began to wonder what Jay had done to the car because it was not burning oil when they sold it to him. It was clear Jay was now in trouble in a big way.

Jay wanted to pray about the mess he was in, but somehow all he could think of was that if he had only listened to God in the first place none of this would have happened. He remembered that under the Old Testament sacrificial system there was really nothing specified to atone for intentional sin, and now Jay understood why.

Three days passed and driving the big gray car he had once treasured had become like carrying the albatross of the ancient mariner. Every time he pulled into the gas station he was reminded of his stubbornness that had gotten him into this mess. He finally prayed with all of his heart for the Lord to forgive him and to help, even if it meant having no car at all. As Jay arrived home after that prayer and got out of the car, out of nowhere a beautiful butterfly landed on his left shoulder. Jay's heart leaped with joy and his eyes were filled with tears. Somehow Jay knew the butterfly was a sign from the Lord, and everything would be just fine.

Within a week of that evening when the butterfly landed on his shoulder, Jay changed cars. This time he was back in a little six-cylinder car that averaged ten miles a gallon more than the gray car and Jay was very happy to have it. But there was more. After the deal was completed and the car was delivered, Jay learned the salesperson who helped him out was himself a pastor only temporarily working at the car dealership for a few weeks. After the night the agreement was made, Jay never saw that salesperson again and as far as he knew the salesperson never knew Jay was a seminary student.

When seminary classes resumed at the end of the summer, Jay sat down with his

New Testament professor and shared his agonizing experience and the wonderful results the Lord was able to redeem out of the disaster Jay had embroiled himself in. Jay's New Testament professor, one of the wisest people Jay had ever met, asked if Jay had learned anything from all of this. Jay admitted he had a lot to learn about following the leadership of the Lord. Then Jay grinned and described what a fantastic experience it was watching the Lord bring everything together. "I'm not looking for trouble," Jay told his professor, "But bring on the next problem; I love to watch the Lord work."

Exult in our tribulations advises the apostle Paul. As Jay found in the midst of his problems, when we repent, the Lord is faithful. But not all problems are due to our own actions. Some are the ministries in which the Lord would have us serve. The principle is the same. When the normal human response might be to give up and become hopelessly depressed, Christians are called to take hope and look for whatever the Lord might do next. Exult in the tribulations, and Christian life becomes the adventure the Lord promised it would be.

Prayer

Dear Lord, give us the strength and the courage to exult when we find ourselves in our next tribulation, and when those around us question how we can face the problems in life with such hope and joy, help us to share your love. In Christ we pray. Amen.

Victory

Call

Let all who would proclaim the glory of the Lord gather this day in worship and praise.

Prayer

Dear Lord, there are so many times in life when we would so like to know why events happened as they did. Help us today to remember that no matter how things look in the world around us, the eternal victory will be yours. In Christ we pray. Amen.

Scripture

Romans 8:37-39

Hymns

"Jesus Savior, Pilot Me"
"Come, Ye Disconsolate"

It was two o'clock on Sunday morning as the telephone began to ring. The hospital chaplain, accustomed to calls at all hours, snapped out of a deep sleep almost instantly and alertly answered the phone. It was the head nurse in the emergency room at the hospital and even though this particular chaplain was not on call, the nurse was asking if she could come in to help with a family who had just lost their infant son to SIDS. Of course the chaplain was quick to respond to help a family face the unexplainable agony of losing their infant child with no warning and no way to prevent the loss.

As the chaplain arrived at the hospital emergency room, there was anger and grief in abundance. The baby's father doubted that the chaplain should even be there since God let this happen to their child. The mother screamed and then her voice slid into the unmistakable wailing tones of grief. From everyone the question came at the chaplain, "Why did this have to happen?"

The sunrise was beginning to show on the eastern horizon before the parents, family, and chaplain finally left the hospital. With the funeral set at the end of the week to allow time for tests to be run to confirm the cause of death, the chaplain could visit with the family several times. At first the bitterness was still very apparent. The chaplain never even suggested to the parents that there were any answers for Baby Del's death. Sometimes the chaplain just listened for an hour at a time as the grieving parents alternated from telling of each little development they saw in Del to angrily telling God the death of their baby was not fair.

Now the family had arrived at a second recurring theme. The first was "why did this have to happen" and the second was telling God the loss of their baby was not fair.

As the chaplain drove back to the hospital from visiting the baby's family, the thought came to her that God might be very familiar with the claim death is sometimes not fair. After all, Jesus, the son of God innocent and without sin, was humiliated and brutally put to death on a terrible Roman cross. "Yes," the chaplain thought, "God must certainly understand the parents' feelings behind their accusation that their child's death was not fair."

Why indeed does a child ever have to suffer and die? To most adults, the thought of a child's death is simply not acceptable. To have lived a full life and had the normal chances to experience and contribute to the world makes death more tolerable. But for an infant or a child who has never even had the chance to really know the fullness of life, dying is unthinkable.

Today, children suffer from accidents, disease, poverty, and starvation. And today, children suffer from acts of abuse and brutality, even at the hands of those who should be loving and protecting them. And we ask, "Why God?"

Or how can it be that a nineteen-year-old college honors student can be so exhausted from finals he falls asleep at the wheel on the way home for the summer and is killed in the crash that results from his car veering off the road?

And why does the young father of three suddenly develop muscular dystrophy and have only a few years to live while across town an up and coming businessman plans to commit suicide because he has broken up with his girlfriend?

How could God let a wonderful and loving biblical scholar and his wife die in a senseless car accident caused by people drag racing on public streets?

Or how could God let a seminary professor who had walked with and witnessed faithfully for Christ throughout all of his adult life and whose warmth and genuine Christian love has touched the lives of many many pastors and church workers become afflicted with Alzheimer's disease?

Or how can people who are hateful and deceitful sometimes seem to win in the various contests that are a part of life while those who are loving and caring often pay the price for much of the deceit in the world?

The simple and honest truth is that we do not have very good answers for any of these questions we might like to bring before the Lord. The chaplain, who has agreed to perform the funeral for the tiny infant, will have to struggle to find some meaningful way for God to use him to open the door to beginning the healing process for the parents.

In our modern world we have become so used to the scientific method and so confident in our intellectual abilities to solve problems that questions that do not lend themselves to answers within our lifetimes tend to be somewhat unnerving. But unnerving may not be so bad if it serves the purpose of helping us see that the universe is in the hands of God and God is by nature beyond the comprehension of our human minds.

How can we adjust to questions of this magnitude with no answers? We can adjust to these questions by clinging to our faith. In the eighth chapter of Romans, we hear a promise for all of those believers who can step out and have faith. The apostle Paul is telling us that in Christ, there is nothing that can come between us and the Lord. Nothing! Nothing here means not anything in the present world or even death itself can come between us and the Lord.

Not accidents nor devastation, not Alzheimer's nor SIDS, not AIDS nor cancer, not even death itself can separate us from an eternity with the Lord. We may not have answers to some of the questions, but we have been given God's assurance Christ will be the ultimate victor over death for all of eternity.

Prayer

O God, sometimes we would like to understand the world in our own terms instead of your terms. Forgive us, Lord, when we have focused only on our losses and overlooked the victory you promised. In Christ we pray. Amen.

Law vs. Spirit

Call

Let all who seek to proclaim the grace and mercy of the Lord gather this day and worship the one true and everlasting God.

Prayer

O God, help us to understand the difference between trying to live by the law and living by your spirit. The world would call us to live by the standard of doing only what is required, but you call us to live by your standard of love. Show us the way Lord. In Christ we pray. Amen.

Scripture

Romans 7:6, II Corinthians 3:5-6

Hymns

"O Spirit of the Living God"
"Jesus, Priceless Treasure"

As Cindy stood up and walked over to the podium to begin her training session, she saw the same eagerness in the faces of her audience that she had seen so many times before. She herself had been in an audience for the very same purpose not all that many years ago, so she knew the pressure these people were feeling to make their sales quotas. But how could she help them understand?

Cindy's own story is not unlike that of many other Christians. Eight years earlier she had been out in her sales territory trying to cram seven days worth of sales calls into a five-day week. Her territory covered some seventy miles north to south and almost a hundred and fifty miles east to west. Her two predecessors had lasted a total of three years between them. One quit after a year, and the other had a heart attack. After her first six months in that territory, Cindy had thoughts of quitting before she had her own heart attack or breakdown or whatever it was she felt was coming soon if something did not change.

Cindy's life was hectic and stressful. She was up by four thirty A.M., and usually on the road by six. Her car was now equipped with the latest radar detection devices she could find. After accumulating two speeding tickets in only six months from the little "jerkwater towns" as she called them, she could not afford a third.

Cindy's first stop in her day was usually at the office where she worked on orders and in general took care of whatever other matters required her attention. Cindy tried to make her first sales call as near eight fifteen as possible and then tried to be back home before seven P.M. Needless to say, Cindy's marriage was paying a price for all of this, but she figured it would only be until she got ahead and then she would work fewer hours.

Eight years ago, Cindy, who had been raised in the church, and her husband had become Christians. Cindy, who was very serious about whatever she did and known to be a person who kept her word, knew her whole life was going to explode if something did not change. In her heart, Cindy gave the Lord "one chance," and if God blew it, she would never trust God again.

To Cindy, one chance meant honestly giving all she had to the Lord to see if trusting God would make any difference in her life. She began praying every day and even set aside a devotional time when she first got to the office. What slowly began to happen over the next six months or so amazed even Cindy.

At first Cindy noticed how the people around her were changing. She actually began to like the customers she called on. Cindy had trouble believing how much nicer they were all becoming.

The real shock came for Cindy when she was stopped again for speeding in one of those "jerkwater little towns." She knew she had been speeding, and she knew the officer was only doing what had to be done as part of his job. But the officer only gave her a warning ticket. The officer explained they knew Cindy was a regular visitor through their town and Cindy was just trying to earn a living. Then the officer asked Cindy nicely to please slow down and understand the slower speed limit through their community was only to try to give the local drivers a safer chance to cross the highway. In a moment of personal revelation Cindy thought to herself, "How could I have been so self-centered as not to have respected the simple request of these people to slow down and give them a chance?" Next thing Cindy knew, she heard herself honestly apologizing and promising the officer she would try to slow down in the future.

Slow down was exactly what Cindy did. For Cindy, it was as though she had just realized what a wonderful world she had all around her and the radar detecting unit she had depended on so desperately became a symbol of the insanity from which she was recovering. These weren't "jerkwater towns" she was passing through; they were communities where people, just like her, lived with their families and friends, and when she respected them she no longer had to try to beat the system so she could speed.

But how could she keep her sales calls up by slowing down? Cindy had been taught the more calls you make, the more sales you can complete. What Cindy discovered was that as she culti-vated her customers by genuinely caring, she did not have to make as many calls and her sales continued to go up as she was given greater and greater shares of their business. It wasn't because she called on them more often, but because Cindy had earned their confidence and respect.

The final truth came out one day in a simple comment made by one of her customers. "Don't know what's happened to you these last few months, but I'm sure glad you're feeling better about life. You're the best sales rep we've had in a good long time." Right then Cindy knew God had taken her up on her challenge, and it had not been everyone around her changing; it had been her.

The Lord had given Cindy a new spirit. All her life she had tried to live by the rules and even manipulate and bend the rules when necessary to accomplish what she felt had to be done.

Cindy had learned what the apostle Paul was writing about in our passage today. For a Christian, living by the spirit goes beyond the letter of the law. The law had set the slower speed limit on the highway in the little community through which Cindy traveled. Cindy slowed down, however, not because of the speed limit, but because she cared about the people living there and felt they deserved her respect and cooperation. Were she to speed through the town and injure someone when she could easily have avoided it, Cindy would feel terrible.

Like Cindy's experiences with speed limits, God has called us to love and respect the people in the world around us. We are called to love and respect others not because there are laws protecting the personal and property rights requiring it of us, but because we genuinely care and respect God's children. There are no guarantees loving others will produce the sort of business success Cindy experienced. Loving others to receive success is not Christian love anyway; it is manipulation. Living life according to the spirit will, however, guarantee a richness to life that could make one wonder if everyone were to live by a spirit of love, would we need laws at all?

Prayer

Dear Lord, thank you for the blessing of your holy spirit to help us learn to love one another. Help us to grow into living in the spirit that we might proclaim the good news of Christ for all the world to hear. Through Christ we pray. Amen.

Andrea and Carlos

Call

Let all who would call upon the Christ as their Savior and their Lord come together this day and lift the joy in their hearts in praise!

Prayer

Dear Lord, as we gather together today, help us to know that your love for us is real, but help us not take for granted that you are also the righteous almighty God of all the universe. Lord, help us to be more responsible children to your call upon our lives. In Christ we pray. Amen.

Scripture

Matthew 21:33-46

Hymns

"Trust and Obey"
"Holy Spirit, Truth Divine"

For fifteen years, Andrea, Carlos, and their children had worked hard to build the reputation of their family restaurant until now they were known by all who lived in the western half of the state and by most who traveled through the area as having one of the finest places to eat in the country. Located in a nice small town on a major U.S. highway, the restaurant was often full of people from at least two or three states.

Their restaurant, which could seat a little over two hundred guests at one time, was not elegant, but it was quite nice with a warm homelike atmosphere. "The ACE," as they called their restaurant, which stood for "Andrea and Carlos serving food with excellence," was not large when they opened it, but with good food and good service, their business had grown over the years. A little at a time, as they could afford it, Andrea and Carlos had purchased the best and most complete preparation equipment they could afford to keep their kitchen as modern, clean, and efficient as possible. Obviously, their investment had worked well.

For almost ten years the people in a very similar community about fifty miles to the west had been trying to persuade the owners of the ACE to open a second restaurant in their little town. Another major U.S. highway passed through their area, and they had done everything possible to convince Andrea and Carlos a second ACE would be as successful as the original. After ten years of resisting and a long family meeting, Andrea and Carlos finally decided to build a second ACE restaurant there.

There was great excitement on the day of the groundbreaking, excitement that remained evident all the way through construction until it reached a peak on the day the new ACE opened. Andrea and Carlos had spared no expense to equip their second location with the very best and finest furnishings and kitchen facilities. They had taken their years of experience and focused all of their knowledge of fine food preparation into planning what many who saw it considered the best designed operation of its kind in the country. Everyone was pleased with the new restaurant.

During the construction period, Andrea and Carlos had carefully selected and trained a new staff to run the second ACE. Several months of work had gone into teaching the new staff the preparation and service methods which had made the original ACE so extremely successful. On opening day, as Andrea and Carlos greeted the guests and observed their staff in operation, they were very pleased with everyone's performance. They were confident the new ACE was going to be in capable hands.

After only a few months of operation however, it became clear to Andrea and

Carlos something was wrong at the second ACE. There seemed to be plenty of customers, but the receipts indicated barely enough income to cover the operating expenses. No one wanted to believe it could be happening, but it appeared as if someone must be skimming money or stealing food. Andrea and Carlos agreed it was time to take action.

The first course of action was to send Thomas, the day kitchen supervisor from the original restaurant, over to observe and try to help bring operations back under control. When Thomas arrived at the new restaurant, however, he received no cooperation and was actually told directly the new ACE was not like the original and things were just done differently here. One of the assistant managers, upset with the way Thomas was interfering, suggested Thomas did not belong in their restaurant and should go back where he belonged.

With Thomas having failed to accomplish any changes, Andrea and Carlos decided to send Linda, their eldest daughter and a managing partner in the overall operation, over to the new restaurant to see what she could accomplish. Linda had the authority to hire and fire managers and knew the overall operation from start to finish. Surely she would be able to sort things out and get the new ACE back on track.

Linda no sooner walked into the kitchen than the hostility began. She was called names, the staff laughed at her, and finally an angry kitchen supervisor waved a large chopping knife in the air and asked Linda if she knew what happened to people who stuck their noses in where they did not belong.

Taking none of this as a joke, Linda left and phoned her parents to report the situation at the new location was now totally out of control and to ask what she should do next. Deeply saddened by how their vision for the new restaurant had gone so far astray, Andrea and Carlos told Linda to return home as quickly as she could. The next course of action would be to contact their attorneys and the sheriff and proceed with removing and filing charges against the renegade staff who had lost track of who they were and the job they had been hired to do. Then Andrea and Carlos would start over with new people to see what they could accomplish in the new restaurant.

Naturally we are disappointed and angered by those who would steal and cheat the decent and honest people who have tried to provide opportunities for employment. We are outraged by those who would threaten and commit violence toward the very people who have trusted them and given them opportunities to work and provide for their families. But whether we realize it or not, the same principles of dishonesty and rebellion that anger and outrage us are very much at work when the church, created and commissioned by Christ to reach out to the poor, the wounded, and the lost in our world, becomes comfortably institutional and self-serving instead. The same behavior on the part of the employees that caused Andrea and Carlos to remove them and seek out others to get the job done is involved when we as the church care only about our own personal interests and activities and refuse to reach out and care for the needs of others who stand wounded and in need before us in the community.

Both the parable of the landowner and the experience of Andrea and Carlos remind us we must always be open to honestly examining whether we have truly been faithful personally and as church communities to the task Christ has given us to accomplish. God has promised, if we will remain open and seek the leadership of the Holy Spirit, the Lord will remain with us and keep us moving toward the work we are to be about.

Prayer

Dear Lord, first we thank you for having called us to be a part of your church. And we thank you for being so loving and patient with us when we continually have fallen so short of your commission for the church today. Lead us into the full service in your kingdom you would have us be about. In Christ we pray. Amen.

Authority

Call

Come, let us lift our voices in song and loving praise before the Lord God Almighty.

Prayer

Dear Lord, as we gather this day, help us to be more aware of the special blessing you have given us, that through

Christ we are members of your holy family. Help us to be more aware also of the authority and the responsibility you have called us to shoulder as your loving church in today's hurting world. Through Christ we pray. Amen.

Scripture

Acts 15:1-11, 22-29

Hymns

"Praise the Lord Who Reigns Above"
"Joyful, Joyful, We Adore Thee"

The voices continued to get louder and louder as the discussion before the church missions committee continued. The proposal had been made to establish a mission effort in one of the most rundown ghettos of the city. It was to be a multilevel effort with a clinic, employment assistance center, an educational unit where a G.E.D. program could be carried on, and a combination preschool and day-care center. None of these, however, were at the center of the controversy. The controversy focused on a proposed chapel service, or more specifically, the suggestion an offering should not be taken during the chapel services for the first year. Instead, Zee was suggesting a voluntary offering box be located someplace out of the way where people who wanted to give could do so privately and those who did not feel able at the moment to give would not be made to feel uncomfortable by an offering taken publicly during the service.

To this point, the intense communications on the subject had been rather moralistic and marked with a good bit of homespun theology. As strange as it might seem, none of the committee members had brought a Bible with them so the scriptures they were using in support of each side tended to be extensively and persuasively paraphrased.

Zee's strongest points were there was an opportunity to give in private and he used Jesus' criticism of public displays centered around the offering and the passage saying the right hand should not know what the left was giving. Armanda countered with Jesus' praise for the widow who gave the mite and the idea it was good for the new mission to help support itself.

Underlying those positions, however, was the real issue at hand. To open a mission effort without public offerings had simply never been done by their denomination before and Armanda's group doubted the church had the authority to make a change of that magnitude with no specific scriptural text to support the move. Zee put it very simply when he said how it seemed to him the mission would be giving to the needy with one hand while they were taking from the needy with the other. It just did not seem right to him.

Finally, tempers cooled and it seemed clear to all involved they would not arrive at an answer on this particular evening. The committee adjourned committed to each member spending as much time as possible in prayer and study on the proposal and meeting again next week at the same time. They also agreed they would work at coming to an answer on the proposal in the spirit of Christian love and not by trying to drum up support in sheer numbers just to win the issue.

The week seemed to fly by as everyone

sought very hard to come up with some sort of clear understanding of what the Lord would want them to do with the new mission. Even as the committee was entering the meeting room, the atmosphere was unmistakably different. There would be no heated discussion this evening, but there could be some answers.

No sooner had everyone taken their seats and the meeting was called to order by the chair than Armanda asked permission to speak. Noting with a grin that everyone had brought their Bibles with them this time, Armanda confessed she had an apology to make to Zee. She had been reading through the four Gospels when it struck her that time and time again Jesus had done wonderful things for people without taking up an offering. She realized Jesus did not attempt to take the place of the temple, but there were times when he fed thousands and could easily have taken a collection. So maybe a voluntary offering would be acceptable for a year until the mission was able to get solidly established.

Zee asked to speak as soon as Armanda finished. Zee admitted maybe he had been a bit stubborn also and the passage of how the Lord loves a cheerful giver had been running through his mind all week. How could new believers be taught to give cheerfully if the mission did not give them a chance? He too was sorry he had gotten a bit out of line the week before.

Then Cho, the committee chair, spoke up and explained he had also found something during his time of study and prayer that he wanted to share with everyone. Cho reminded the committee how one of the real issues the week

before revolved around whether or not the church had the authority to make changes and do things differently than they may have ever been done in the past. He asked everyone to join him in looking at the fifteenth chapter of Acts. Here, Cho explained to the committee, Paul was working out the issue of whether Gentile men becoming Christians would be required to undergo circumcision as the law and tradition had required. Under the law, circumcision was the key identifying symbol of being numbered among God's chosen people. Shockingly, Paul contended that circumcision was not to be required and the newly formed church went on to uphold Paul's view on the issue.

Cho said it seemed to him if the church, after much prayer and consideration, was empowered by the Holy Spirit to have the authority to set aside a law of the magnitude of circumcision, the church after prayer and seeking the leadership of the Holy Spirit today had the authority to decide whether an offering should be public or private in a new mission effort. With understanding nods of approval, the committee unanimously agreed with Cho. The committee now felt empowered to recommend whatever it believed was best for the mission, and chose to seek the opinions of those who would be attending the new mission.

What a valuable series of lessons about the nature of Christ's ministry and the authority God has entrusted to the church through the leadership of the Holy Spirit. With each new generation and the onslaught of modern technologies have come new and challenging issues facing the church. If the church is to remain God's redeeming instrument in the world today, we must remember we have not been left to fend for ourselves. In God's infinite wisdom, we have been given the support of the scriptures and the loving guidance of the Holy Spirit. The challenge is whether we will do as the early church and the committee did in spending time in study and prayer to seek the leadership of the Holy Spirit, or if we will try to arrive at our answers on our own.

Prayer

Dear Lord, give us the strength and the wisdom to move beyond our own limited insights to seek out your guidance and leadership through the Holy Spirit. There are so many challenges before the church today and only your leadership can guide us to becoming the witnesses you intend for us to be. In Christ we pray. Amen.

Grace

Call

Let us give praise to the Lord that we who are sinners have through God's mercy and grace been made welcome into the house of the Lord.

Prayer

Dear Lord, help us today to more fully accept your love and your grace. In so many ways we still shelter deep in our beings the idea that in some small way we are worthy of your grace. We give you praise, Lord. Through Christ we pray. Amen.

Scripture

Ephesians 2:8-10

Hymns

"Let Us Plead for Faith Alone"
"Love Divine, All Loves Excelling"

There are probably fewer concepts contained within the New Testament more foreign to the human personality than the idea of our eternal salvation being the result of God's grace. Most of us are

skeptical, at the very least, of anything that seems to be ours without a reasonable explanation.

For example, you read the following ad in the newspaper: "Millions of dollars will be given to anyone who will accept the money and agree to use it to help the poor." As a lark you call the number listed and put your name on the list. Within the hour your doorbell rings and when you open the door there stands a team of attorneys. The attorneys explain how you are to receive twenty million dollars and all you have to do is use the money to help them reach the poor. Your task will be to seek out the poor and convince them to send their names and addresses to these attorneys. All who send in their names will in turn receive money when they agree to the same terms you have just agreed to accept.

Most likely one of your first questions would be, "Why me?" "Because you believed enough to respond," comes the answer. But you argue that you have done nothing to deserve this sort of gift.

"What could you possibly have done to deserve twenty million dollars anyway?" comes their reply. The whole arrangement seems crazy, but as the attorneys leave you are holding a check for twenty million dollars and a promise that if you run out of money helping them reach the poor there will always be more available to you.

Wondering if the check is real, you decide to take it to the bank and deposit it. Before you actually make the deposit, you ask the teller to call and verify if the account the check is written on has enough money in it to cover the check. They call and the check is perfectly legitimate. So you deposit twenty million dollars in your account.

The condition you agreed upon when you accepted the check was that you would use the money to reach the poor. But how exactly does one reach the poor?

You get in your car and drive to a disadvantaged neighborhood where you stop at the first house you come to and go up to the door. When you try to explain to the person who answers the door that all they have to do to receive a lot of money is send their names to the address you hand them and people will come to bring them money in exchange for telling others to send in their names, the door is abruptly slammed in your face. When you knock again, you hear the voice inside warning you to leave or they will call the police.

Over and over again you encounter the same skepticism. Why? Because our human nature tells us it is unlikely anyone is going to give away anything of great value for nothing. Such an ar-

rangement is simply not believable. People running con games use the "something for nothing" approach, not legitimate people.

Another facet of human behavior that makes God's grace such a challenge to accept is price. We want no part of being indebted to anyone, not even God.

When Tom and Sherry moved into a different neighborhood, Alice, their new neighbor, thought it would be nice to take the couple a cake as a welcoming gift. Sherry received the cake and invited Alice in for a visit. When Alice left, Sherry told Tom how as soon as she could get her kitchen things unpacked she would make Alice a pie and take it to her as a way of saying thanks for having welcomed them to the neighborhood. Tom laughed and assured Sherry no response to Alice's welcome gesture was expected other than to pass it on and be willing to join in welcoming the next new neighbors into the neighborhood. Sherry wouldn't listen to Tom and said she was not about to let an act of kindness go unrewarded. Sherry was also not going to enter the neighborhood feeling indebted to Alice.

Or how about the time when Toby went to the hardware store to order a part to fix the faucet in the kitchen sink. After the counter clerk had looked up the part, gotten it from the warehouse area and written the ticket, Toby discovered he was a dollar short of what the part was going to cost. The clerk looked up from his ticket at Toby's troubled face and said, "Ah, don't worry about it. You're in here all the time and we'll make it up on something later." Toby thanked the clerk, went straight home, got the dollar he owed the store, drove straight back, and gave it to the clerk. Toby was not going to be beholden to anyone.

With all of our human logic, what among everything we possess could we possibly think would be worth the price of our eternity to God? Some suggest it is not things or possessions we earn our eternity with, but through our actions. Like many parents say to their children, "If you are good this morning, we'll all go to the park and have a picnic this afternoon."

The argument that we could earn our salvation with our behavior sounds more reasonable until we think about the whole picture. It is one thing to tell our children we will have a picnic for them if they are good for a few hours one morning. It is quite another matter, however, to believe a person could possibly manage to be "good" for an entire lifetime. In all probability, most parents would admit they had to stretch the definition of "good" just to consider the children's behavior acceptable for one morning, and the thought of a whole day or a lifetime of good behavior is simply unimaginable.

So what would one call such a decision by a parent to accept the borderline morning behavior of their children in order to allow them to go on the afternoon picnic? Most would likely call it "grace." Why then do we have such a struggle accepting that God, our heavenly parent, would want to provide some way for us to receive the unmerited blessing of eternity?

Human pride has one more characteristic within it that makes grace hard for us to accept. Our culture is full of sayings about people being "self-made" successes. Only when we finally accept the reality, that no matter how hard we try or have tried, our salvation is in no way the result of our own personal efforts, can we truly grasp the magnitude of the gift God extends to us in salvation by grace. When we receive salvation only by grace, then, as the apostle Paul tells us in our passage today, not one person can boast salvation was received as the reward for their personal efforts or genetic heritage. Eternal salvation results only when we as sinners accept God's lovingly extended grace.

Maybe it would help others to understand Christians are not claiming we deserve the love God has extended to all who will accept it if Christians wore a button which said something like, "Imperfect and saved only by God's grace. Care to join me?"

Prayer

Dear Lord, you know us so well, including our sins, and yet you have made every effort to reach us with the message of your salvation. Help us to move beyond our pride and accept your grace. Through Christ we pray. Amen.

Signs and Wonders

Call

Let all who would worship the almighty God, creator of all the heavens and the earth, bow down this day in loving praise for the Christ who has called us to be God's children.

Prayer

Dear Lord, as we come together this day, touch our hearts with a new awareness that you are truly God, with all of the wisdom and the power of the universe. In Christ we pray. Amen.

Scripture

I Corinthians 2:4-5; 4:19-20

Hymns

"Amazing Grace"
"Rock of Ages"

The local hospital had offered a special training session designed to help the volunteer chaplains become familiar with the latest information available about AIDS and other highly contagious diseases. As the session came to a close, three of the pastors attending decided to go to the hospital cafeteria and have a light lunch together. Collectively Sherry, Charles, and Mort represented a good many years of ministry. Individually, however, the pastoral ministry was Mort's second career and he was very much enjoying only his second year in full-time service.

As the three sat enjoying a cup of coffee after lunch, Mort asked what Sherry and Charles thought about miracles. The topic being somewhat controversial amongst the clergy, both Sherry and Charles carefully asked what Mort was thinking about on the subject. Mort said, "Well, if you won't laugh, I'll tell you," and went on to relate his story.

As it happened, Mort had a church member in the hospital that very day. He had gone by to visit with the member before coming to the training session. The church member was a wonderful lady about sixty-five years old and the doctors were battling an infection in her abdomen. Mort said he wished he could do what Jesus and the apostles had done and just reach out and heal the woman. Cautiously Sherry asked if Mort thought that might be what God had wanted him to do. "I don't know," confessed Mort. "I wanted so much to just reach out and take her hand and know she would be healed, but I did not want to look silly, I guess. God doesn't heal much like that anymore."

"I don't know about that," said Charles. "If you two won't think I'm crazy and you'll not tell anyone, I'll tell you something that happened to me not too long ago." Both Sherry and Mort agreed and Charles continued.

As it happened, Charles had gotten to the hospital late one Saturday evening to make a follow-up visit on a church member who was in critical condition in ICU. As Charles left the ICU he thought he would make a second visit to another member suffering from congestive heart failure in a room on the fourth floor. Charles related how as he stood riding up in the elevator he realized how totally exhausted he was and how he would have to keep the visit short. In fact, he wondered why he was making the visit for his energy level was so low he had nothing really left to give.

Charles quietly eased the door to the member's room open and asked ever so softly, "Chet, are you awake?" "Sure," came the reply in a tone that expressed the joy one feels to have a visitor in a lonely hospital room. "Come on in here and have a seat." Charles assured Chet it was quite late and he did not have time to stay long, but he wanted to know how Chet was doing. "The doctors tell me not too well, preacher. Nothing seems to be working this time and . . . ." Chet's unfinished sentence said what Chet could not say with his words, that he might not survive at all. Chet smiled and asked, "Do you have time to pray for me preacher?" "Sure," said Charles, all the time thinking in his own mind Chet could not have known how exhausted and drained he really was. But if it would make Chet even a little more comfortable, Charles would pray for him. Charles gently reached over and took Chet's swollen hand and just as he began to pray, Charles felt something like a bolt of energy pass through him. In his heart Charles was thinking "God, how can this be happening now when I am totally exhausted?" When Charles looked up, he saw Chet's smiling face and heard him say, "You know I've been healed, don't you?" "Yes I know," was the reply.

Charles looked at Sherry and Mort and said, "They sent Chet home the next day. I couldn't believe it. I was so tired I could hardly move and God goes and does that. I think God just wanted me to know how unimportant I really am. As I rode the elevator back down, I leaned against the car wall and said, 'Thanks God. I just love it when you keep me humble.' "

Sherry grinned and said now that Charles had told of his experience, she had had something very similar happen only about a month ago. Molly, the matriarch of a wonderful family in her church had been in the hospital for some rather serious surgery. Everything went well until suddenly Molly's kidneys began to shut down and the doctors were having no success at all in getting the kidneys to start up again. Molly's condition was growing very serious.

By the time Sherry arrived most of the family had arrived and were visiting in the room. Most hospitals have regulations about how many people can be visiting at any one time but as was the case with Molly, when the situation is very grave the rules are waived to allow the family to be present should the patient die. Molly was not conscious as Sherry came in, but the family greeted Sherry warmly. Finally Sherry knew she was supposed to pray for Molly. The family all joined hands and Sherry reached over and held Molly's foot. As was the case with Charles and Chet, Sherry felt something happen and when everyone opened their eyes and looked up, Molly was awake, alert, and the doctors soon reported her kidneys had suddenly started working again and she was out of danger.

Mort could tell from the way Charles and Sherry told of their experiences that neither was totally surprised by them. Charles and Sherry admitted they had seen similar miracles before, but it simply was not wise for them to be talking about miracles a great deal and both insisted what they had shared today should go no further. Mort agreed he would say nothing, but it certainly gave him something to think about.

The difficult thing to comprehend is what could possibly have happened to modern Christianity to cause Charles and Sherry and others like them in the church today to feel the need to be so careful about publicly sharing the experiences they have had with the healing power of God. Of course the greatest miracle of all is still the miracle of salvation, but God had promised Christians they have not been left alone in this world and God's power will still be present and demonstrated through signs and wonders among those who would give witness to the gospel of Christ. Maybe there is more wisdom than we realize in James 4:2 when it tells us "we have not because we do not ask."

Prayer

Dear Lord, we thank you for caring for us even when we do not recognize your love and attention is present. Give us the eyes of faith to know your will and the courage to ask that your power might be demonstrated so others may come to believe. In Christ we pray. Amen.

Crosses

Call

Let all who seek to serve the Lord and who would accept their cross to give witness of God's love, gather this day and worship.

Prayer

O God, help us this day to have a greater understanding of your call upon our life. Help us, Lord, to grasp how the price you paid for us on the cross demands the very best we have to give in return. In Christ we pray. Amen.

Scripture

Matthew 16:24, 26:36-46; John 12:27-28

Hymns

"Must Jesus Bear the Cross Alone"
"Nothing Between My Soul and My Savior"

The pastor's appointment schedule for the next few hours that afternoon was booked with people coming in for personal counseling. The pastor had met before with each of the members coming in today and had been praying all week for guidance on how to best help each person.

The first person on the schedule was Gretta. Gretta had been married to Otto for a good many years and through most of that time it was common knowledge Otto had a tendency to drink a good deal more alcohol than he needed to be drinking. It was ironic, however, that as much as Gretta complained about Otto's drinking, she freely admitted she herself kept the house stocked with a case or so of whiskey for Otto.

Over the several years Gretta and Otto had been members of the church, Gretta had met with the pastor on several occasions about her problems with Otto's drinking. Each time she would fatalistically refer to Otto's excessive drinking as just being her "cross to bear," she would question how and why God could have let Otto's drinking happen to her. In her most dramatic moods Gretta would even compare the agony she was experiencing to the agony Jesus must have gone through in the Garden of Gethsemane when praying with the disciples before being arrested and taken to the cross.

The pastor's second person on the schedule would be Randy. Randy was a middle-aged salesman who had a wonderful personality and a considerable knowledge of his product line. Randy's reason for visiting with the pastor was his job. Randy felt he was being treated unfairly and that his boss was holding out on his sales commissions. This would make only Randy's third time to visit with the pastor over the past three months, but Randy had already made it quite clear that as he read the scriptures, he had no other choice but to honor those in authority over him and since his boss was not an honorable person, Randy saw his job crisis as a cross he had been called to bear. When the pastor had suggested Randy might want to look around for another job, Randy reminded the pastor there were no jobs in today's workplace for middle-aged

men and he had to stay where he was if he was going to support his family.

The third appointment on the schedule that afternoon was a family with two teenage children. The children, both now in high school, had been in trouble at school for skipping classes and their grades were close to the failing level. The children who were only nine months apart in age, had each received a car for their sixteenth birthday. It had been shortly after each received their car that the disappointing behavior had begun.

The reason the parents had started coming to counsel with the pastor was because they had heard some rumors their children might be getting involved with a group of young people who were heavily into using and trafficking in cocaine. Again, just the week before, the couple had sat wringing their hands as they wondered why God had given them this terrible cross to bear.

As the pastor had been preparing for the afternoon of counseling appointments, it seemed as if the following Sunday would be a good day for a sermon entitled, "The Nature of a Cross." The topic lent itself to a natural three-point outline.

The first point would be "Those who are called to a cross are innocent." Crosses are not the result of improper behavior we may have committed nor are they due to our own neglect. Gretta could not claim Otto to be her cross when she had contributed so willingly to his drinking problem and had never seriously sought help or tried to change her contributing behavior. Randy could not call his situation a cross because he allowed his own insecurities and fears to prevent him from confronting his employer or from searching for another place of employment. And the parents of the two teenagers were hardly without culpability as they provided the temptations of the unrestricted use of automobiles without providing reasonable supervision and guidance for the children.

True crosses are instead the result of standing firm in our witness for the Lord. The person who is asked to cheat in a business deal but refuses and is then fired for standing on the principle of honesty has accepted his cross. The person who refuses to become involved in the gossip circles in the community and is thus excluded and not considered part of the club has accepted her cross. The person who refuses to participate in the worldly celebrations surrounding church holidays and who is shunned and given the label of being a religious fanatic has accepted his cross.

Point two would be "Crosses are voluntary and accepted of our own free will." On this point the pastor would have to be very careful. Gretta, Randy, and the parents had all questioned why God had imposed such burdensome crosses upon them, yet in reality their situations had resulted in large part from some of the choices they themselves, knowingly or unknowingly, had made and were continuing to make. But true crosses are accepted because we wish to serve the Lord. Like Jesus, we may have some fears and trepidations about the crosses we are called to accept, but we will accept them because we trust and love God.

And the final point would be, "Crosses are redemptive in nature." Jesus died on the cross that we might be redeemed from our sins. Our crosses will not save others, but they may well point others to the Christ who will. None of the three who claimed to be enduring crosses had any redemptive qualities about their situations. All three could have redemptive qualities, however. Gretta could begin to stand firm and help Otto face and conquer his drinking problem. Randy could stand firm and hold his boss responsible for the unethical behavior. The parents could begin to stand firm and confront their children before it is too late. Redemption always comes with a price, and we must be willing to pay it.

Suddenly the intercom buzzed and the pastor knew Gretta had arrived. Although the sermon sounded like a good one, because the examples were too current and confidential it was hardly one to be used right now. Like many sermons, however, the outline would be set aside for the present, but not lost. The pastor would carefully work on it and when appropriate examples were finally found and the time was right, it would be delivered.

Prayer

Dear Lord, help us face the responsibilities of life you have given us and give us the guidance and the wisdom to be able to recognize the true crosses you would have us to bear. In Christ we pray. Amen.

Finishing the Race

Call

Come! Let the weary in the Lord rest. Let those who would serve the living Christ know the love and peace of God. Let us all join together in worship and praise for the Lord God Almighty hears our prayers and the Holy Spirit is with us even now.

Prayer

O God, you did not call us to an easy carefree life; you have called us to give witness to your mercy and love for all the world to see. Give us the strength, Lord, and give us the courage to finish our days true to your word. Through Christ we pray. Amen.

Scripture

II Timothy 4:7-8 (Hebrews 12:1-2)

Hymns

"For All the Saints"
"Of All the Spirit's Gifts to Me"

Many communities across America celebrate the various holidays during the year with parades. There is just something special and uplifting about parades with the marching bands, the floats and vehicles of every sort decorated to fit the occasion. Some parades even include contests for the best floats in various categories not so much for any monetary rewards but for bragging rights and for the added enthusiasm the float contests tend to generate.

Not long ago, one such community parade was planned to kick off the Christmas season. It was to be a night parade and many different businesses, community agencies, and civic clubs had floats entered in the float contest. This parade had one of the largest turnouts and some of the finest quality floats for a Christmas parade anyone in the community could remember.

As the judging was taking place in the hour before the parade was officially to start, the excitement level was almost as high as it would be during the parade itself. All the float lights were turned on, and the various costumed characters were all in place on the floats giving the full effect of each float's message.

Finally the float winners were announced and the parade was underway. It was at this point that a most remarkable thing happened. Even though the course of the parade route had been set so the judging area and start of the parade were only about a block from the city square, the top award-winning float ran out of gas just as it reached the square. With the parade already in progress, there was no possible way for any float to stop and refuel. The builders of the winning float had simply miscalculated how much fuel they needed for the judging period and the rest of the parade. As a result, their float won top prize in the judging area, but very few people along the parade route ever had the chance to see the wonderful message it had to convey.

Of course, running out of gas for a parade float certainly represents no critical life or death situation. In fact, the float was designed and entered by a young and energetic civic group and, even though they were disappointed by the mishap, they also found it mildly amusing and a terrific learning experience. The same float building crew intended to be back for the next parade with an even bigger and better float.

But failing to be prepared to complete the entire course ahead of us is not always such a lighthearted matter. For example, to have even a small military unit run out of fuel, as a part of an army engaged in heavy combat, could not only be fatal to everyone in the unit, it could also lead to the loss of the battle or even of the whole war and eventually have some potentially serious consequences for an entire defeated nation. Or for a surgical staff to fail to do adequate preparation and not have the proper supplies and equipment readily available to complete an operation, could obviously result in a very serious, if not fatal, situation.

The apostle Paul knew full well the importance of not only doing one's best but of also being committed and prepared to complete the tasks we set out to do. The images Paul uses in this passage are from the great athletic games of his day. Paul writes Timothy about how he has fought the good fight. Winning or losing is not all there is in athletics despite the ever present "winning is everything" slogans we tend to hear from the business-oriented professional athletic community today. In Paul's day, athletics was not the business it is today and thus athletes could focus on the need for personal honor, integrity, and on doing one's ultimate best. Winning or losing was not the true standard; dignity belonged to those who had hon-

orably done their very best in the contest. Paul is not saying here that he was victorious in everything he attempted, but he is saying he has lived his life with honor and he has given his very best for the Lord.

And Paul, seeming to sense the end of his own life could be near, states how he is approaching the finish line of life with honor. The modern Olympic games are replete with stories of athletes who, even while suffering terrible pain or having significant injuries, insisted on finishing their race. Even with winning totally out of the question for these injured athletes, the honor of having done their best, injuries and all, meant completing the race and complete it they would. On many occasions, as the lone limping obviously hurting athlete has crossed the finish line, the fans in Olympic stadiums have responded with thunderous applause truly recognizing that this is a victory of a very special sort. Paul writes Timothy that for him, the finish line is in sight now and he is going to reach it with honor. He will finish this most important race called life and he will finish it with the honor and dignity that belongs only to those who have done their very best.

Paul then makes his third point to Timothy. Paul will finish the course of his life having truly kept his faith to the very end. Most who serve the Lord would like to come to the close of their lives and be able to join Paul in saying they had kept the faith. Life is full of many temptations and the closing days of life are certainly no exception. The temptations may be totally different from those in our younger years, but they are temptations none the less. The words of Paul call us to do our personal best before the Lord; to run the race of life to the very end without ever giving up; to hold true to our faith no matter what our circumstances; and to remember in our hearts Christ will lovingly have the last word.

For us to do any less we would be like the Christmas float that ran out of gas. And like the float, we might even win a few awards along the way, but if we do not have commitment to keep our faith and witness bright all the way to the finish line, who is going to notice? There is foolishness in the long-distance runner who starts like a flash and soon fatigues to the point she cannot even finish the race. Life is not a sprint race, but a long-distance run. And winning is not everything. Honor, personal integri-ty, and faithfully giving our best for the Lord all the way to the finish line of our race as Paul suggests are still what really matter in life. If we will do these things, we can rest assured the Lord can and will take care of the rest, and one day we might well have the honor of joining Paul in saying confidently we have run our race and we have been faithful to the very end.

Prayer

Dear Lord, sometimes we tend to be so very shortsighted in life. We mean well but we burn ourselves out before we are halfway done with our task. Lord, help us to sort out what is important, and to use our energies wisely that we might both do our best and finish our race. Through Christ we pray. Amen.

The Desert

Call

Come! Let all who would seek the leading of the risen Lord, join our hearts in song and praise.

Prayer

O God, as you guided Moses through the struggles and hardships of life to eventually lead your children out of Egyptian bondage, we ask your leadership in our lives today, that others might know you are God. Through Christ we pray. Amen.

Scripture

Acts 7:20-36

Hymns

"See How Great a Flame Aspires"
"As the Sun Doth Daily Rise"

In the minds of many, Moses is such a larger than life personality it is almost hard to imagine he was only human like we are. But just as the scriptures describe for us the spectacular events surrounding the Exodus, they also share enough about the man Moses to leave little doubt he was indeed very human. The same scriptures that tell us of Moses' role in the confrontation with Pharaoh, the parting of the Red Sea, and the delivery of the Ten Commandments also tell us of Moses' impetuous nature and his insistence he was not a good speaker and upon God allowing Aaron to speak for him.

In our passage from Acts we have outlined something we do not always remember about this extraordinary life God used to accomplish so much for the people of Israel. Moses' life was essentially divided into three distinct periods of forty years each.

Moses, having been raised by the Pharaoh's daughter, was forty years old when he first understood God's intent to use him to lead the people of Israel out of Egypt. At forty, Moses would certainly not have been considered to be old, yet neither would he have been considered in the prime of his youth. At forty, Moses was at the point in life where it would have been very natural to assume if something is going to be accomplished, it is time to see to the task yourself. For many even today who have reached the age of forty, Moses' willingness to accept God's assignment to lead Israel out of Egyptian bondage followed by his taking matters into his own hands and personally undertaking the task of starting a revolution seems like a pretty reasonable approach. Before we hasten to become too critical of Moses' direct methods, we must remember the scriptures do not tell us about God having given Moses any plan to follow in accomplishing the Exodus.

And that leads us to the second forty-year period in the life of Moses. After Moses took matters into his own hands and killed the Egyptian guard, it became necessary for Moses to flee into the desert to escape Egyptian punishment for his deed. And thus began forty years of living in the desert land called Midian.

It is this second forty-year period Moses spent in the desert we tend to overlook. We know Moses married and eventually had two sons. We know he worked hard and did relatively well for himself. But beyond these few images of Moses during this middle forty-year period we know very little.

Moses simply did not record and share his innermost thoughts about life as did David or Solomon. But this second forty-year period must have held for Moses many times of questioning. It is hard to believe that Moses did not question both himself and God. Had he really heard God telling him to lead the children of Israel out of Egyptian bondage? If he had heard God, then what did he do wrong or why did God fail to multiply his efforts and bring about the Exodus? If God really intended to use Moses, why did God leave him out in the desert all these years?

It is this forty years Moses spent in the desert seemingly out of the picture as far as God was concerned that should be both challenging and comforting to us today. We live in an age when television has trained us to expect the resolutions to life's problems in thirty minutes, an hour, the length of a movie, or at the very most in the few days it takes to complete a miniseries. Forty years is really not very comprehensible to us. As adults we might consider goals like college requiring four years or maybe adding on various graduate programs and occasionally extending that to ten years, but even these long-range plans pale by comparison to Moses' forty-year period in the desert.

But God's time and ways are not always like ours. For example, God's promise to Abraham to one day make a nation of his offspring was not fulfilled during Abraham's lifetime. But the promise was fulfilled just as God's plan for Moses to lead the Exodus would come to pass. We are called not to think for God but to be faithful.

Personal times in the deserts of life can be times of great spiritual growth if we will trust God. We can observe some of Moses' personal growth as we see him at the age of eighty years facing the burning bush and once again being told God intends for him to lead the Exodus. Moses at eighty is no longer ready to take on the Egyptians singlehandedly. The elder Moses is not even sure how to tell his own people the time for the Exodus has come or that God has called him to lead them. Moses is a very different person after forty years in the desert.

It is very important we remember it is this eighty-year-old Moses who was the heroic figure we are really thinking of when we recall the Exodus. The heroic Moses is the same Moses who earlier, while he roamed the desert region around Midian, probably wondered many times if God had completely forgotten about him. This is the same Moses who had once decided to take matters into his own hands killing the Egyptian guard and who probably reflected many times of what wonderful things God might have been able to do through his life had he not been so impetuous and messed things up so badly. It is the same Moses, who once fled Egypt fearful of the Pharaoh's power, who will now boldly confront the Pharaoh of Egypt filled with the confidence God will be in control of whatever is to happen.

There is a very good chance that at least once in our Christian walk we will each have the opportunity to spend some time in life's deserts. It may not actually be in a physical desert like Midian, but it will have all of the earmarks of a spiritual desert and we will know where we are when we are in it. And hearing the lessons of Moses will not necessarily make our stay in the desert any shorter or any less disagreeable, but it may help us keep our faith strong.

Deserts seem to be a part of life as God would have us experience it. No one wants to hear their stay in the desert might last forty years, but forty years was how long Moses spent in the desert and look at the great things God still had planned for him afterward. Deserts do not lend themselves to quick simple answers that solve everything and make life all better. Instead, deserts are times, if we will cling to our faith, when we can personally experience how, no matter how bad everything seems to be around us, we can still totally and completely trust God. Deserts can be times of great change and great spiritual growth. Who then, when we think about it, would not accept time in the desert?

Prayer

Dear God, we do not like the hard times in life, but we are grateful you can use even these times to build our faith and our relationship with you. We praise your wisdom and mercy Lord, and ask you to help us to grow in our faith through whatever conditions you would take us. Through Christ our Lord we pray. Amen.

Joy in Heaven

Call

Let all who would proclaim the wonder of God's mercy and grace come together in the house of the Lord for worship!

Prayer

O God, as we gather today to come before you and worship, lead us to new and stronger understandings of the wonderful gift you gave to us through the cross and the resurrection. Help us to see more clearly how precious is our membership in the family of God. Through Christ our Lord we pray. Amen.

Scripture

Luke 15:3-10 (Possibly most effectively read as part of the devotion)

Hymns

"Victory in Jesus"
"Amazing Grace"

It can be a wonderful adventure for a Sunday school or Bible study class to occasionally tackle questions that may not have routine answers and have to do a little research as a group. For example, an adult Sunday school class started its study one Sunday morning with the question, "What was the most important accomplishment of Jesus during his years of ministry before he was crucified?" Bibles of many different colors and cover designs were opened as over a dozen people began to look for what they considered the most likely answer.

"It's gotta be the miracles!" one fellow said. "But which one?" came the answer. First the class talked about the various healing miracles. The group discussed several of the miracles and wondered if one was spiritually more important than another. Finally someone mentioned the raising of Lazarus from the dead had to be the ultimate healing miracle and thus Jesus' most important accomplishment.

Then, in a very uncertain voice, someone asked if maybe the times Jesus had cast out demons might not be more important than the times he healed people. Again the pages began to rustle as the class discussed passages pertaining to times when Jesus had cast out demons. The discussion soon moved to whether casting out demons was a greater act than healing the sick or raising Lazarus from the dead.

No sooner had the debate begun between healing and the casting out of demons than someone asked about the time Jesus calmed the sea and walked on the water. Again the pages rustled and again the discussion intensified until someone suggested maybe the Sermon on the Mount and Jesus' teachings were his greatest accomplishment. At this point the time for class to be over had arrived and everyone agreed to think about it and finish the discussion next Sunday morning.

It is amazing what happens when people really get involved with a question like this one. All week long the class members were thinking and working on the question. Married couples talked over breakfast about which might be the most important. Class members called each other on the telephone with new ideas just to see how their ideas sounded to some of the others. Some of the class members even brought the challenging question up on their lunch breaks at work and before they knew it the people they worked with were adding their opinions to the mix. By Friday afternoon one class member had even invited a person from work to come to Sunday school that Sunday to join in the discussion and to see how it all came out.

Finally Sunday morning arrived. It had been a good while since anyone could remember being so involved in Sunday school they could hardly wait for class to start. People had even come early and were standing around in little groups of two or three hard at work stating and explaining their personal choices. After the opening prayer, the class discussion that followed would have made a seminary professor proud.

Healing, raising the dead, the casting out of demons, demonstrating authority over nature, and Jesus' various teachings all seemed like well-qualified choices, and each certainly received an eloquent defense from one or more of the class members. But discussions that eventually seem to have no clear solution often more or less dry up as everyone comes to realize the answer may honestly be a matter of personal opinion. About the time this Sunday school discussion seemed to be reaching the drying-up point, someone mentioned something about "joy in heaven." The whole Sunday school class came to a thoughtful silence. "Well, didn't Jesus

say there would be 'joy in heaven' over something?" came the restated question.

Once again the pages rustled as everyone searched. "Looks like Luke 15 may be it starting at about verse three." someone said. Sure enough Luke 17 was the passage they were looking for and everyone took special note of verses 7 and 10 which spoke of the "joy in heaven" over even one sinner repenting. (This might be an appropriate time to read Luke 15:3-10.)

Almost as though an unspoken wave of understanding had flowed over the class, everyone seemed to see the obvious at the same time. No passage mentioned any joy in heaven over any of the healings Jesus had performed. Nor was joy in heaven mentioned over the raising of Lazarus from the dead. And there were no mentions of joy in heaven when Jesus calmed the angry sea. The scriptures seem to reserve the mention of "joy in heaven" occurring only on those occasions when Jesus led sinners to repent from their sins. The joy in heaven comes when God's precious lost sheep are found and returned to the Lord's fold.

Finally the Sunday school class agreed on what Jesus' most important accomplishment during his ministry before the cross might have been. The physical healings Jesus performed were certainly wonderful, but the people who were healed eventually aged and died. And again, although the message of Jesus' power over death was made very clear in the raising of Lazarus from the dead, eventually Lazarus also died. And there were certainly more storms on the sea, that goes without saying. But those people who repented and turned their lives over to following Christ received an eternity not limited to this world or to this lifetime. Those whom Jesus rescued and returned to God's fold have become citizens of a new kingdom, and they are not limited to the bounds of any earthly measure. It seemed very clear to the class, one of the most special events in all of creation is when we as sinners repent and give our life to Christ. After-all, as even one sinner repents, the angels in heaven celebrate.

That Sunday school class struggled very hard with its question and through the leadership of the Holy Spirit they rediscovered one of the most important understandings of the Christian faith.

So often we take the magnitude of the gift of God's saving grace for granted and fail to realize how incredibly special and wonderful salvation really is. The repentance of even one sinner is so special even the heavens celebrate. Do we?

Prayer

Dear Lord, we thank you for loving us so much you came seeking us even before we realized we were lost. We thank you for calling us to repentance and for your grace and mercy. Lord, renew our sense of wonder in our being a part of your kingdom that we might share our joy with all we see. Through Christ we pray. Amen.

Scriptures

Call

Let all who would seek a living relationship with the risen Lord join together this day and lift your voices in song and praise!

Prayer

Dear Lord, so often we have taken our eyes away from the resurrection and thought only in terms of the cross. Lord, touch our hearts anew with your presence that we might once again remember your promise to walk with us in every moment of every day as we serve you. Through Christ we pray. Amen.

Scripture

John 5:37-40; II Timothy 3:14-17

Hymns

"Fairest Lord Jesus"
"Hope of the World"

Several years ago, upon learning in the news of former President Harry Truman's death, a high school history teacher shared a personal regret regarding President Truman. It seems the teacher lived and worked in the Kansas City area and occasionally visited some friends who lived in Independence, Missouri, the community where the former President resided and where the Truman Library was located. One day the teacher's friends casually mentioned the Trumans were family friends and asked if the teacher would like to stop by and visit Harry and Bess

Truman. Modesty, shyness, and a concern for the Truman's privacy prevailed and the teacher turned down the extraordinary opportunity. The teacher went on to share how it would not be until several years later, after reading some of President Truman's writings, that he came to realize how much the former President of the United States enjoyed visiting with students and teachers. Of course now, with the President's death, the opportunity was gone forever and the only way to know the thoughts and views of Harry Truman was through his writings. There are few things more tragic in life than missed opportunities.

In our passage today, we see Jesus confronting a very similar situation. For generations the children of Israel had prayed for their Messiah to come. For generations the Jews had studied the scriptures intently to prove themselves worthy before God until that day when God would finally send a Messiah to restore the glory of Israel. The rabbis throughout the land had carefully taught the messianic prophecies just as certainly as they had taught the Mosaic Laws. Among the devout, it would have been rare that a Jew did not know of God's promised Messiah.

Now Jesus walked among them and they would not receive him. Jesus, the Emmanuel, God with us, was the answer to the prayers of generations, yet the rabbis and priests would not accept him. Instead the religious community continued to teach and preach about God's promised Messiah yet to come. Instead, the Temple and synagogues continued to study the laws passed on to them by Moses so the Jews might be found worthy in the day of the Lord.

In retrospect it is easy to see an incredible opportunity was missed by the leadership of the Jewish religious community during those brief years of Jesus' earthly ministry. It might even be easy to jump to some fairly judgmental conclusions about the priests and rabbis regarding their personal level of insight and their genuine understanding of the very scriptures they were teaching. How could they possibly have been willing to settle for reading and studying the scriptures when they could have personally known and talked with and interacted with Jesus, God incarnate?

But the person looking back in retrospect almost always has the advantage. It is easy for us today, looking back through the eyes of faith, to realize how illogical the choice was to reject Jesus in favor of the scriptures. It is easy for us, who live in an age of instant global communications technology, to take for granted our access to firsthand information from leaders of every sort from whatever part of the world they may live and work. But are we really that much different than the Temple leadership of Jesus' day?

In our passage today from the Gospel of John, Jesus point-blank accused the scribes and Pharisees of religiously studying the scriptures as their source of salvation rather than seeking out and developing a personal living relationship with the Christ. This accusation has a frightening and ominous tone of warning in it sounding across the nearly two thousand years for those of us in the church today. Jesus said the purpose of the scriptures was to point to a living saving relationship with him. The apostle Paul, in our passage from II Timothy, tells Timothy that studying the scriptures will lead one to a salvation based on a living dynamic faith in the Lord Jesus Christ. Yet how many of us today are tempted to spend more time learning "about" Jesus than we spend "with" Jesus in prayer? How many of us would rather seek out the missionary journeys of Paul or item the various conflicts of the early church found in the book of Acts than we would spend time lifting our families, our churches, and our neighbors to the Lord in prayer? Or how many of us would rather share the dramatic salvation story of the apostle Paul on the Damascus road than we would share our own personal witness of the Lord's salvation in our life?

Several decades ago there was a lay evangelism movement that reached across denominational lines and focused on Christians sharing their personal relationship and experiences with Christ. Some churches, while conducting this week-long program, insisted participants bring their Bibles to church for Sunday school and worship services so they could follow along during the various studies. But when the evangelism efforts began through visitation, the Bibles were to be left at church and those visiting were encouraged to share their personal experiences of faith in Christ. How many of us today would rather just search the scriptures?

Of course this is not an either-or situation, but both. As Jesus, the apostle Paul, and the entire Reformation movement would try to help us understand, the scriptures are an invaluable guide for leading us to a vital dynamic living faith relationship with our risen Lord and Savior Jesus Christ. Nothing less

than this level of relationship is strong enough to withstand the pressures that can oppose the church. It was this living faith relationship with Christ that sustained Christians through the Roman persecution. It was this living faith relationship that sustained the early believers as they journeyed throughout the world to share their faith with everyone they met. It was this living faith relationship that sustained the church through the almost fifteen hundred years it would take for the printing press to make it possible for everyday people to afford and own a copy of the Bible. And it is this same dynamic living faith relationship that Jesus calls each and every Christian to receive today.

It is easy for us to look back on the rabbis and priests and wonder what could they possibly have been thinking to have chosen to study the writings about Jesus and to have passed by the chance to know the Lord firsthand. But today we must also ask ourselves if we are open to allowing the scriptures to lead us to that same living relationship with Christ offered to them, or will one day others look back on us and wonder in amazement, what could we possibly have been thinking?

Prayer

Dear Lord, sometimes we are so inclined to think about everything and we are slow to just accept you into our life. We open our souls before you today and ask you to know us and to enter fellowship with us in all that we do. Lead us in our everyday activities and use us, Lord, to celebrate your mercy and love. Through Christ our Lord we pray. Amen.

Pigpen

Call

Let each one whose heart has known the mercy and forgiveness of the Lord gather this day and lift the joy of your soul in praise.

Prayer

Dear Lord, we gather today in praise of the redeeming work you have so mercifully done in our lives. Hear our praise, Lord, and use your handiwork to give hope to a hurting world. Through Christ we pray. Amen.

Scripture

Luke 15:11-32

Hymns

"Come Back Quickly to the Lord"
"Where Charity and Love Prevail"

No parable Jesus gave us speaks more directly or eloquently to the hearts of many Christians than this one about the prodigal child. The parable tells us of a young man who chooses to prematurely collect his inheritance which he then promptly wastes on wild living. Eventually the young man realizes the destitute condition he finally reaches is the just reward for his behavior and elects to accept the consequences of returning home where at least as a servant to his own family he will receive adequate food. However, upon returning home, the prodigal is not received as a servant, but rather is lovingly forgiven by the father and restored to being a child in good standing and a great celebration ensues.

This parable is so familiar some in recent years have begun to explore every conceivable detail of the story in an effort to discover something new and meaningful to hold the attention of today's Christians. For many, however, there is something very special and wonderful about hearing the gospel of Christ through this parable again and again, no matter how many times the story is told.

For there is something unique about the way the parable of the prodigal child truly does seem to speak volumes of truth about the very nature we all seem to share as humans. Hardly a one of us who has truly come to know God's mercy and grace can read this passage and not remember a time in our life when we too, like the prodigal, were bent on following our own paths only to find them hollow and empty. As we revisit this parable, we are reminded of at least one time when we, too, found ourselves sitting in the midst of despair because of our choices and wondering if we would ever again be forgiven and accepted back into the family of Christ.

We are reminded of times of failure when everything seemed to have gone wrong—times when relationships had failed and we were not sure we could stand the agony we were feeling—times when our finances had failed and we were not sure we could face our friends and neighbors or how we might answer our creditors as we tried to pick up the pieces—times when our decisions affected our children and we felt like the spotlight of failure was focused on everything we had ever done wrong as parents.

Or there are the times when we have set our goals in directions that were not God's directions for our lives! Times when we sold our souls to achieve worldly success only to discover we had nothing left but hollowness and emptiness in the midst of great wealth; times when we were determined the victory would be ours whatever the cost only to discover after winning the victory the price was too high; times when we focused our lives on what we thought we wanted and had to have to make us happy, only to discover after we finally obtained it that it wasn't really what we thought it would be and certainly did not bring us happiness.

And what about those times when we have chosen to tell God we were going to live life our own way? Those were times when we rebelled against the training of our youth; times when we were finally old enough to make our own decisions in life and were free to turn our backs on the old-fashioned outmoded Sunday school life-style our elders tried to lead us into living; times when the choices we made led into such high levels of stress we thought we would never survive and wished only to have the chance to be washed clean of the mess we had made of our life so we could start over and live by the old-fashioned values of loving, respecting, and caring for others.

Nor can we overlook those who one day come to realize that in their attempt to avoid mistakes and failures in life, they have done nothing at all with the talents with which God has blessed them. For those, who most of their lives had thought of themselves as the obedient children of God, to suddenly realize they too, through their inaction, had strayed from God's will into a pigpen, just as certainly as did the prodigal, the message of the gospel is just as meaningful. The parables of Jesus make it abundantly clear we will be held accountable for what we could have done but did not, just as surely as we will be held accountable for what we have done.

We could go on and try to describe the sorts of situations that make up the pigpens in life in which we find ourselves, but this is the beauty of parables and poetry. Parables and poetry both tend to speak through images that allow us each one to interpret the parable or poem through the eyes of our own experience and personality. Hear, if you would, a poetic restatement of the good news of the parable in the poem "Pigpen," by J. R. Wilson.

"Pigpen"

The pigpen is a remarkable place,
A smelly, dirty hole in space.
Most of us choose to sit in its midst,
Our pride, our image, our wills we insist,
Are all we need to live and survive,
So we get in the pen through our stubborn drive.

Sometimes it looks remarkably fair,
To those outside who aren't in there.
Sometimes it has money and style;
Sometimes success, ahead of others by miles.
Sometimes it's lined with failures and divorce,
Poverty, disease, promiscuities of sorts.

Almost everything possible can be there.
One thing seems common, to feel no one cares.

But the pigpen really is an incredible place,
The last place of all in time and space,
You'd expect to find a loving God's Grace,
In a pigpen, what a remarkable place!

The parable of the prodigal truly does speak to the heart of the human condition. And the promise—if we are willing to climb out of the pigpen and come home, God is willing to lovingly forgive us and to restore us as children in good standing in God's family—is real. For those who have experienced God's love firsthand, well, we each have a personal pigpen story to tell if you need a word of encouragement. For those who might be in a pigpen today, it's time to come home. God is waiting.

Prayer

Dear God, there are not enough words to truly thank you for the love and forgiveness you extended to us while we were still sitting in the pigpens of life. We give you our praise and ask that you help us share the good news of Christ with others who need to come home. Through Christ our Lord we pray. Amen.

The Movie

Call

Come, let us worship in the house of the Lord. Let the rich and the poor, the mighty and the humble, the old and the young, let us all—from whatever background—come together to worship and bring praise before almighty God!

Prayer

O God, help us truly hear in our hearts today of your wonderful love and concern for each and every one of us. Help us to move beyond the values of our culture and time to see the infinite worth and value we each hold in your eyes. Through Christ our Lord we pray. Amen.

Scripture

Mark 9:2-13

Hymns

"Lord of the Dance"
"Open My Eyes, That I May See"

Wouldn't it be exciting if somehow, out of the clear blue, we were asked to help make a movie based on the scriptures—a movie dedicated to being as true as possible to both the events and the personalities we find described in the scriptures? A large foundation is funding the project, so operating capital is not an issue, and even though the movie is intended for public release, neither is profit. The purpose for the movie is to faithfully present the scriptures with the hope the public audiences will hear God's message through the movie.

As one of the consulting directors, you meet some pretty high-powered and famous talent. The producer, one of Hollywood's most noted, has already brought together some of the finest production people in the world to shoot and edit the movie.

The script, mostly taken directly from the scriptures themselves, is already in hand and you find it quite impressive. No fictitious romantic interests have been added or implied just to spice things up a little. The few liberties that have been taken seem only to keep the flow of the movie going and add very little other than background to the scripture text.

But casting and special effects are a different matter. These are both yet to be done, and you will have significant input in these two areas as well as the actual direction of the movie. And it is in these areas where the snags seem to have already occurred.

For production reasons, the first scenes to be shot will be the difficult ones requiring special effects to be added later. The first scene scheduled is the transfiguration with Jesus, Peter, James, John, Elijah, and Moses.

As you arrive on location in Jerusalem, the actor who will play the role of Jesus has been selected. He is an Israeli actor with dark skin, dark eyes, longish dark hair and he stands about five feet nine inches tall. The question everyone is working on as you arrive is what sort of people to look for to play Peter, James, John, Elijah, and Moses.

What would Peter, the spiritual giant who was such a crucial part of the early church, have looked like? And what of James and John, the two Jesus called

"the sons of thunder"? What sort of people were they?

Just for inspiration, the production team takes a trip out of Jerusalem up to the Sea of Galilee. There, along the shores, you observe the fishermen and their boats. The faces of the fishermen, even the younger ones, are dark and weathered. Their bodies are tough and strong, used to long hours of hard work. Their clothes are simple and practical, nothing that would interfere with their labors. You sense these fishermen share a feeling of community and yet they are also quite independent. It seems a bit incredulous that Peter, James, and John, three important spiritual leaders in the early church, could have come from among fishermen such as these. These are ordinary people, used to honest, hard work, not highly trained religious leaders skilled at evangelism and church building. Yet it was fishermen, just like these, whom Jesus called to follow him and whom God used to spread the good news of Christ to the world.

Back in Jerusalem, the decision is made that the production team will look for rugged, strong, ordinary fishermen types to fill the roles of Peter, James, and John. Attention is then turned to the sort of actor needed to play the part of Moses. The historical background people open the discussion by describing Moses based on what information is provided about him in the scriptures. Moses was eighty years old at the time the Exodus began and he provided leadership for the children of Israel until his death at the age of one hundred and twenty. By Moses' own description, he was not an effective public speaker and having spent from the age of forty until he was eighty as a herdsman in the desert regions around Midian, Moses was most likely weathered and tough. As for his clothing, like the fisherman along the Sea of Galilee, Moses probably dressed in a practical and functional way rather than in the fine garments of that time.

Except for his having lived to be one hundred and twenty years old, Moses seems surprisingly ordinary, especially to anyone who may have seen previous Hollywood portrayals of the man. And when the background people turned their attention to the type of actor needed to play Elijah, the description is similarly unspectacular.

Now back to reality for a moment. Taking an honest look at the people God chose to use, as scriptures actually record them to have been, is really what doing this little exercise about making a movie was all about. So often we tend to let ourselves think the people chosen by God in the scriptures were in some way special and not like the ordinary people of the world. This view is simply not borne out in the scriptures. Over and over again we hear disclaimers of inadequacies from the very people God chose to call. Moses considered himself a poor public speaker. Isaiah spoke of himself as being unfit and unworthy to serve God. Even Abraham literally fell over laughing at the idea God could use a hundred-year-old man and a ninety-year-old woman to bear a child and begin a nation. And the descriptions of the people Jesus called to serve God in New Testament times are clearly descriptions of the same sort of imperfect ordinary people we are today.

The point is not that the people in the scriptures were extraordinary and special or that they were capable of doing God's work on their own. Instead, the point is that God's presence, call, and blessing are what made the difference and the special events we read of occurring around these scriptural personalities were a result of God's handiwork, not the handiwork of the chosen people.

So if today we have those feelings of being unworthy to serve God and feelings we are not capable of the kind of works recorded in the scriptures, we are right. But take heart; God asked only that we be willing to serve, not worthy or capable, and through the Holy Spirit, God will take care of the rest. Isaiah's unclean lips were cleansed for him, and Abraham and Sarah did give birth to Isaac just as God said they would. So the question becomes simply whether we are personally willing to present our lives to the Lord, just as we are and without reservations, and will we accept wherever and however the Lord would choose to have us serve.

Prayer

Dear Lord, sometimes we hide behind the mask of being ordinary and lacking in gifts. Today we accept your call to all of us, even the ordinary people whom you will bless and use in very special ways as part of your kingdom. Use us, O Lord. Through Christ we pray. Amen.

Needs vs. Wants

Come, let us gather together, all who would give praise to the Lord God Almighty, creator and sustainer of the universe!

Prayer

O Lord, so often in our daily lives we forget that you are God. Today, give us the spiritual eyes and ears to hear your word for us from the scriptures. Focus our hearts, Lord, not on life the way we would want it to be, but on life under your lordship. Through Christ our Lord we pray. Amen.

Scripture

Philippians 4:10-21

Hymns

"Here I Am, Lord"
"Blessed Jesus, at Thy Word"

You receive a letter, you open it, and there on the first line in sharp clear print is the word, "Greetings!" With just that much information to work with, you really have no idea how you would react to the letter, do you? We need to place the message "Greetings" within some sort of context for it to be effective.

If you had the letter in your hand, you would probably be able to see the letterhead and know if it perhaps were from the IRS, suggesting an audit, in which case you might feel one way; or possibly it is a notification you had just won the grand prize in a multimillion dollar sweepstakes, in which case your reaction could be of a slightly different nature. The context of a message can very much alter the very nature of the message itself.

The importance and effect of the context on the message can certainly be significant for some passages in the scriptures as well. Verse 19, for example, taken out of context as it often is, can be made to sound as if Paul is promising God will provide a life of worldly luxury for all believers. Although it is certainly within God's power to provide for believers in luxurious worldly ways, is Paul, when we put this verse back into context, possibly giving us a greater lesson in faith for our day?

First, in the very broadest sense of context, let's take note of the circumstances within which Paul found himself as he was writing Philippians. Paul composed this epistle from within a Roman prison with full knowledge his own death was soon to come. If one remembers Paul is incarcerated, then Paul's references to abundance and to all of his needs being cared for seem wildly out of place. But then again, maybe they are not.

In verses 10, 11, and 12 of our passage, Paul writes of having learned to be content whatever the level of circumstances in which he finds himself. Whether his environment be of abundance and comfort or whether it be humble and stark, as it was in the Roman prison, Paul was doing just fine.

Paul's freedom to be who he was under any circumstance and in any environment is a real challenge to our western thinking today. Some suggest Paul lived in a much simpler and easier time than we do in our high-tech fast-paced world and the difference between poverty and wealth then was much less noticeable than today. True, it was a technically less advanced day back then, but humans have changed very little, and class distinctions were as real then as they are today.

But Paul, through his years of boldly living out his faith in Christ, had learned two very important lessons that made it possible for him to write these thoughts to the Philippians. First, Paul had come to realize the difference between "needs" and "wants" in life. Our "needs" list, if we are really honest, is actually quite short and simple. Probably as adults, all we genuinely physically need is adequate clothes to wear, enough food and water, and an adequate place to sleep.

Some defining at this point may be helpful. "Adequate clothing" does not require expensive or currently fashionable styles. Adequate clothing consists of whatever garments are necessary for modesty and warmth. We do not need expensive blouses or shoes or pants or shirts or warmups or whatever. "Adequate" does not even require clothes to be "new" or flawless. It might be a great faith-building experience if every church in the world on one given Sunday made arrangements to meet at a nearby Christian homeless shelter where church members would all trade clothes for whatever was on the racks and then hold a worship service. It might be a revelation how God loves us even when we worship wearing second-hand clothes.

"Enough food" means only that we need enough of the basic food groups to sustain our body. It does not mean we must have expensive, exotic, or fashionable foods, some of which, ironically, may not be good for us anyway.

And an adequate place to sleep can be very basic indeed. It is staggering to consider the wealth we have dedicated to building the homes we feel we "need" to live happy and productive lives.

Now beyond our "needs" come our "wants," and we could compile endless lists of "wants." We can want almost everything under the sun and some things that have not even been invented yet.

The second great lesson Paul had learned is actually a subtle part of the first. The greatest of our human needs is the need to know God and to accept the truth God loves each and every one of us. Once he finally accepted God's love, Paul's whole view of life changed. After all, if we are accepted and loved by God, the creator of the universe and controller of all of eternity, why would we need to extravagantly display worldly wealth in an attempt to gain acceptance from our peers? To use a not completely accurate corporate analogy, if one is recognized, highly valued by and in close contact with the CEO of the company, what's the point of doing things just to try and impress our coworkers in the mail room? And yet how many of us spend more time trying to impress our coworkers than we do talking with God?

Taken in context, Paul's promises of God's faithfulness in meeting our "needs" become as shining beacons of freedom from the temptations of materialism. Remember verse 19 mentions only God's promise to meet all of our "needs" and not all of our "wants." God truly does love us too much to give us all of our wants just as we as human parents love our children too much to grant their every wish.

But far greater than our physical needs is God's promise of an unending, accepting, and forgiving love for each of us. We can have enough food, our clothes can be adequate and we can have a fine place to sleep, but without accepting God's love, we will still be struggling. God's truth is so simple and yet so often we will not accept God's love because it does not make human sense. "There is no free lunch!" some say, yet God's mercy and grace *are* free. Unless we can accept God's freely given love, no amount of persuading is likely to ever convince us Paul was making perfect sense as he wrote in Philippians telling of his abundance while in a Roman prison awaiting a certain death.

Our needs are real and our need to know God can only be met one way. We can try everything the world has to offer to fill our need for God but we will certainly come up short. Or we can join Paul and the Christians across the ages and accept the love God, who knows our every need, freely extends to us through Christ. Which will it be?

Prayer

O God, sometimes we are such rebellious children as we search in every direction but toward you to discover who we are. Thank you, Lord, for loving us even when we have lost our way, and help us know your love and your values in life. Through Christ our Lord we pray. Amen.

What I Have I Give

Call

Let us come together and worship, all who would share their living faith in the Lord.

Prayer

Dear Lord, as we gather together this day to worship, open our hearts to the true nature of faith. Touch us with a new awareness of the blessings we have to share with the world. Through Christ we pray. Amen.

Scripture

Acts 3:1-10

Hymns

"Take My Life, and Let It Be"
"Jesus Calls Us"

Several years ago, not long after their New Testament class had completed the study of Acts, a young seminary student shared a most remarkable dream about today's passage. In the dream the student was walking up to the front door of the seminary chapel. There, just to the right of the door, sat a lame beggar asking for alms. As the student approached from the parking lot side of the chapel and saw the beggar, the similarity to this passage came to mind. With a certain sense of pride and a touch of adventure, the student figured it was time to act on faith and do exactly what Peter and John had done so many years ago.

As the student approached the lame beggar, their eyes met and without a word the beggar extended his right hand palm up to receive the student's gift. In a dramatic voice, the student began to recite, "Silver and gold have I none, but what I have—" and right then the beggar angrily interrupted. "Silver and gold have you none? Who are you kidding! You wear a ring on both hands, you wear fine clothes, you drove up here in a nice car, and you are even overweight. Get out of here! You can't even be honest with yourself!"

Totally stunned and speechless, the seminary student turned and left. Walking back out to the car intending to think about these events, the student began to realize there was truth in what the beggar had said. Later, while telling of the dream, the student smiled and said: "It was my dream. I couldn't believe the audacity of the guy messing up my dream, but he was right."

And how many of us are like the seminary student in the dream, a bit out of focus on who we are and what we have? It is so easy to imagine we might one day be able to walk in the faith like the greatest of the saints. So easy to imagine one day we might be able to walk up to the lame beggar at the door of the temple and extend what we have to him. But then, what do we have?

For Peter and John, what they had was faith. When they told the beggar they had no money, they meant it. Their faith journey through life was without savings accounts, retirement plans, or even anticipated future paychecks. They did not even have pocket change. Peter and John had no money! Their money was not forgotten at home on the dresser or in a checking account with the banks closed on Sunday; they had no money! It is so easy to take their statement casually as we might say we have no money and mean really we have none with us at the moment. Again, for Peter and John, this was not a casual statement. Instead, they gave what they had, their faith in Christ.

Back to our question; what do we have to give? So many times we are tempted to overspiritualize scriptural lessons and when we do we can miss the obvious. There is no attempt in the scripture passage to imply having wealth is morally wrong. Even in the seminary student's dream, the beggar was upset at the student's lack of honesty, not because the student had some degree of wealth.

The real issue is, are we giving of what we have? If we have silver and gold, do we give it to help those in need? If we have the gift of teaching or preaching or healing, do we use our spiritual gifts to serve others? If we have buildings or vehicles or businesses, have we dedicated them to the service of the Lord?

So many times, however, when it comes to giving our wealth before the Lord, we act like some people do with a new car. Around those they are trying to impress, the price of the new car is fairly steep, if not a touch inflated. Around the property tax assessor, however, the new car becomes the least expensive bottom-of-the-line model of its kind.

The Lord does not hold us responsible for gifts and blessings we do not have. We are responsible to the Lord only for what we do have, which means we need to honestly inventory our resources. We need to fully accept that many of us have far greater physical resources than we are often willing to admit. We also need to accept we have each one been given spiritual gifts intended for use in the Lord's church.

Our priorities tend to make the difference when and where we are willing to use and invest our resources. Peter and John's priority was serving their Lord Jesus Christ. Both were experienced fishermen, and both were quite capable of successful careers outside their role in the early church. But both had received important gifts vital to the young church, and both had dedicated their lives to serving the risen Christ. Accumulating silver and gold mattered little to either one of them.

So with the well-placed priorities and faith of two working-class fishermen and the spiritual gifts of the Holy Spirit, we read today about Peter and John becoming two of the pillars upon which the early church was founded—Peter, who tradition holds died a martyr's death in Rome, and John, who is credited for no less than five of the books in the New Testament.

Today, many of us wonder and dream of being able to live and walk in the faith as did these two great saints. As the seminary student, we dream of being able to reach out and extend the miracle of God's healing love to the needy as did Peter and John to the lame beggar at the temple. But when we look at our lives and our resources, where are our priorities? How have we used the blessings God has already given us? If we pulled out our checkbooks and our receipts, what would they tell us about our values in life?

Probably today very few, if any of us, could walk up to the lame beggar at the temple gate and reach out a hand of God's healing. But many of us together could give and help build a hospital. Many of us could carry the beggar to a doctor and together we could cover the medical expenses. Many of us could be a great deal more responsible for serving the Lord in a hurting world with the blessings we have already received. Who knows, once we have demonstrated to the Lord our commitment and faith, one day some of us might reach out a hand to the lame and in faith say, "In the name of our Lord Jesus Christ, stand up and walk."

Prayer

Dear Lord, we would have you grant us so many spiritual gifts, yet we have not always done the very best with the blessings you have already given us. Give us spiritual vision today, Lord, that we might see your leadership and minister to a hurting world with the resources we have to give. Through Christ our Lord we pray. Amen.

The Great Myth

Call

Come into the house of the Lord all who have known God's loving mercy and grace.

Prayer

O Lord, touch us this day with an awareness of your accepting love. Help us to understand and accept that you have known us and loved us even before we were aware of our sins. Through Christ we pray. Amen.

Scripture

Isaiah 53:4-6

Hymns

"I Know Whom I Have Believed"
"All Who Love and Serve Your City"

Every culture in human history has generated or maintained a collection of myths. Even today we seek out and preserve myths from across the millennia of civilization as we struggle to know more about our cultural past. Some myths, like the Isis-Osiris myth used to explain the cycles of nature in ancient Egypt, once played an important part in the human understanding of life. Few in the modern world view these ancient stories as anything other than mythical.

Another group of myths has curiously maintained a persistant role in modern life. For example, Groundhog Day, seen by most as simply entertaining, is still viewed by some as a reasonably accurate prediction for the remaining days of winter. Other myths pertaining to the planting times for crops, hunting, and fishing, or many other areas of our culture, still—although they may have no real basis in fact or predictable results— remain surprisingly influential.

But it is not any of these easily identified myths we are considering today. Instead, the myth we are going to look at and challenge today is far more subtle and pervasive than most would ever consider. This great myth is also far more powerful in shaping our views of life than most would ever think. This myth, simply put, is the idea that surely somewhere in this vast world, someone or some people have succeeded at getting life right and managed to live wonderfully happy lives all on their own apart from the approval of others or even the approval of God.

We can see this myth in action as we observe the way we react to the entertainment industry or the seemingly glamorous life-styles of some we see in the news. Somehow we find it entertaining and believable as the silver screen super spy dashes from one hair-raising adventure to another and goes through one romantic interlude after another never experiencing any noticeable distress or consequences. Or we become so attached to our favorite television sitcom families as they blunder and laugh their way through life always bringing each episode to a wonderful end-of-the-rainbow happily-ever-after conclusion. And we are fascinated by the jets, boats, cars, and beautiful clothes we perceive make up the life-style we often see represented as we watch many of the notables on the TV news.

But, we know, when we really think about it, each of these examples are just flights of fancy and escapism, right? But if we honestly searched through our deepest thoughts and desires, we would probably find what makes all of this so attractive and entertaining to us is our unspoken belief that this great myth is true. Somehow, somewhere, someone or some people really are succeeding at living life according to their own self-centered desires, and they are having a wonderful carefree time in the process.

In order, however, to give even the slightest credence to this great myth, we must ignore a simple but very important three-letter word in verse six of today's passage. The word is "all." God, speaking through the words of the great prophet Isaiah, is making it very clear "all" of us, each and every last one of us, have fallen short of the glory God created us to meet. Not just a few of us, not even all but a very few of us, but every person who has ever lived or will ever live has strayed away from God's plan for our life. "All" is a totally inclusive word intentionally used to let us know God completely and fully understands the fallen nature of the humanity Christ was sent to save.

Isaiah's inclusive "all" should tell us there are no real super spies dashing through life and romantic affairs without experiencing the consequences and side effects of immorality. Isaiah's inclusive "all" should tell us there are no real sitcom-like families who manage to insensitively blunder and laugh their way through life without people experiencing pain, emotional stress, or even deep relationship scars that will require work and healing to overcome. And certainly Isaiah's inclusive "all" should tell us there are no fantasy worlds in which real people live amid wealth and splendor without pressures, anxieties, or tensions simply because we observe the trappings of glamour on TV. The great myth is not true.

There has only been one person who has ever lived a perfect life. There has only been one person who ever made all of the right decisions and never strayed away from God's perfect plan—only one person who cared at the right times, who laughed at the right times, who was quiet at the right times, and who spoke out at the right times. There has only been one person who was totally sensitive to God's leadership and always, without exception, followed the will of God through an entire life without failing even once. Of course that one person was Jesus, the Christ, and we rejected both the example he set and the message of God's redeeming love he was sent to bring us.

Instead, even then, we held on to the great myth we could decide on our own how to be successful and find happiness in life. We preferred either the hundreds or even thousands of stifling religious rules for life the Pharisees recommended on the one extreme; the everything is good if taken in moderation life-style in the middle; or the wild and totally decadent life-style of the sinful nonbeliever on the other extreme; but we wanted none of the loving family images God offered to us in the words and teachings of Jesus.

Isn't it interesting that even thousands of years after Isaiah's words were recorded, or after Jesus walked among us, we are still choosing to believe the great myth is true. Let's try something one more time. The Isis-Osiris myth of ancient Egypt explaining the cycles of nature is not true. Groundhog Day is not based on fact. The great myth that someone somewhere has made it through life without sin or that we can live life our own way and have joy in our life without the mercy, grace, and love of God is not true.

Sounds sort of strange when we put the myths together like that, doesn't it? It seems silly to state the obvious. But temptation is never silly, and neither are the consequences of having yielded to it. "All" of us have experienced sin, but the second half of verse six in today's scripture passage brings the good news that Jesus has taken our sin and washed it away. What an irony! Today there are many who are caught up in the chase after the temptations in life, including the great myth, while at the same time they would declare the words of Isaiah and the gospel of Christ a myth. And this leads us to the ultimate question we each must answer on our own: "What do you say is the truth?"

Prayer

Lord, so often we have each one strayed off in our own directions as we sought what we felt would bring us happiness and joy in life. Thank you, Lord, for understanding our fallen nature and loving us so much you sent the good shepherd to round us up and bring us home. Lord, give us the courage to share the good news of your love with all who would hear. In Christ we lift our prayer. Amen.

Hypocrites

Call

Let all who would lift your voices in praise and song for God's forgiveness, mercy, and grace gather together this day for worship.

Prayer

O God, through the cross you opened the way for each of us to become a part of your family. Today, Lord, as we gather in worship, open our hearts to the ways you would have us reach out and share your love with the world around us. Through Christ we lift our prayer. Amen.

Scripture

Matthew 23:13-36

Hymns

"Dear Jesus, in Whose Life I See"
"We Would See Jesus"

Have you ever just wondered what sort of personality Jesus had as he lived and ministered among us? We seem to speak so often today of God's love, and we tend to focus so much of our time in the church on the many images we have in the scriptures of Jesus as the healer and the merciful one who forgives and restores the broken and sinful hearts around him. There is a warmth we see in the scriptures about Jesus that beckons to each of us to bring our burdens and our sorrows before the cross where we, too, will find God's forgiveness and restoration just as surely as Jesus freely gave it to the sinners who came before him in the scriptures.

However, this is certainly not the only side there was to our Lord's personality. Jesus could also be bold and aggressive when it came to attacking sin, especially when he found it among those who were supposed to be God's messengers and prophets. Matthew gives us a glimpse of Jesus' ability to be strong and outspoken in our scripture passage today.

Boldly Jesus declares the scribes and the Pharisees to be hypocrites. Boldly he pronounces God's condemnation upon both groups for not only failing to enter the kingdom of God themselves, but for having led people astray, who, had they received faithful guidance, would have entered God's kingdom.

And Jesus went on to describe the scribes and Pharisees as being like "whitewashed tombs." They looked good on the outside, but they were full of decay and rot on the inside. In some detail, Jesus describes the religious attitudes that had become a strict set of rules for daily living taught by the scribes and Pharisees. Their strict rules had become hard barriers keeping God's people away from a living relationship with the Lord. Jesus was not afraid, nor was he timid about speaking out against any who would keep God's sheep from their shepherd.

But this episode between Jesus and the temple leaders occurred long ago, and the scribes and the Pharisees and their laws are gone. What possible relevance could any of these matters Jesus spoke against hold for the church today?

Actually the issues Jesus raised can be frightfully relevant. There are probably few Christians who have been a part of the church for any length of time who have not heard the charge that the church is made up of nothing but hypocrites. Non-Christians often contend they are as good as the "hypocrites" in the church, and in some cases they argue their personal life may even be a good bit better. What need then do they have for whatever it is the church has to offer?

You will notice the word "hypocrites" is the same word Jesus used as he was condemning the scribes and Pharisees, who were so sincerely dedicated to living their lives by the highest religious standards. The scribes maintained, clarified, and taught the Mosaic Law, and the Pharisees were genuinely committed to keeping what they believed to be God's laws. It would not really be fair to describe the scribes and Pharisees as being politically motivated or self-centered religious leaders. Although probably any large group may contain some who would fit that description, there were many, especially among the Pharisees, who were devoutly religious people. Yet Jesus accused the scribes and Pharisees of preventing others from entering God's kingdom and he called them hypocrites and whitewashed tombs. How could this be?

Two concepts must be considered if we are to hear the warning this passage holds for us today. The first is "self-righteousness." "Righteousness" in the faith holds the image of being in good standing before God. "Self-righteousness" then suggests that on our own merit or by our own actions and behavior we can deserve or earn a place in good standing before God. The scriptures tell us this is simply not the case. Only Jesus could ever have truly claimed to be worthy of good standing before God on his own merit. Not one other person has ever managed to live a sinless life. Thus, the whole idea promoted by the scribes and Pharisees, suggesting that obedience to the laws was sufficient to earn a person a place in good standing before God, becomes nothing more than a system of "self-righteousness."

The second important concept we need to consider is the New Testament understanding of "sin." The word used in the New Testament for "sin" does not really contain a black and white view of doing what is right or wrong in life. Instead, sin might better be understood as any time we fall short of being what God created us to be. We each have unique talents and gifts and blessings with which we were meant to freely carry out the ministry of Christ in the world around us. Say for example, the rich young ruler Jesus spoke with had chosen to give the equivalent of $100,000 to help feed the poor of Jerusalem. Could that possibly be a sin? Certainly it could. If the rich young ruler was able to have given $200,000 to help feed the poor, but for his own reasons, he elected to give only half the money, then he fell short of being the blessing he was created to be. In the same way because the scribes and Pharisees chose to live by a legalist system, no matter how religious they were in their efforts, rather than seeking out and experiencing the same living relationship with God both Moses and David wrote about so eloquently in the Old Testament, then they too were falling short of what God intended for them and even worse, they were leading others to fall short as well.

And therein lies the warning for Christians of every generation until the Lord returns. We must focus on and seek out the same living relationship with Christ we read about in the scriptures and not allow ourselves to settle for simply being religious or living by a rigid set of laws. The apostle Paul, as the Pharisee Saul of Tarsus, was possibly the most religious person who has ever lived. Yet Paul, by his own testimony, tries to share how being religious is simply not God's plan for us.

If we have chosen the path of being religious, we have chosen the same path the scribes and the Pharisees chose and the non-Christian's accusation we are modern-day hypocrites should ring out as a clear warning just as surely as if Jesus himself were speaking. If, on the other hand, we have found the living relationship with Christ that the scriptures would lead us to have, then surprisingly we might well agree with our accusers. A non-Christian may indeed be living a better life than we are. The good news Christians offer is not founded in our goodness nor set by our example alone. Our message freely and openly declares we certainly do have our shortcomings, but just as certainly our shortcomings have been forgiven before God and theirs can be also. We do not celebrate our own goodness, but rather we celebrate God's wonderful mercy and grace. For we as Christians to make any other claim would certainly leave us open to correctly being called hypocrites.

Dear Lord, sometimes we are so pleased with what you have done in our lives we begin to believe in our own merit and forget the mercy and grace you first extended to us. Help us remember who we really are, Lord, that we might open the door for others around us to know you as we have come to know and love you. Through Christ our Lord we pray. Amen.

Carrots

Call

Let all who would know and share the redeeming love of Christ come together this day for worship!

Prayer

Dear Lord, open our hearts today to the message of Christian love you led Paul to share with us in the letter to the Romans. Lead us to have stronger patience and a greater understanding for those who walk in the faith around us. In Christ's holy name we pray. Amen.

Scripture

Romans 14:1-12

Hymns

"Lord, Speak to Me"
"Where Cross the Crowded Ways of Life"

Once upon a time in the little community of Quarrelsville, there began a tradition among some who lived in the town of not eating carrots. No one quite remembers how this all got started, but one popular story was that when Mr. Wise was interviewed on his one hundred and tenth birthday, almost a year to the day before he died, and was asked what had contributed to his long life, he was supposed to have replied something about never having eaten carrots. A second popular version of how not eating carrots began had to do with a Bible search young Charlie Sharp did one summer many years ago and he discovered carrots were not mentioned in the scriptures.

It doesn't really matter how it all began, over the past fifty or so years the matter became one of serious community concern. Residents of Quarrelsville even began to divide up into their own neighborhoods—people who ate carrots in one part of town and people who did not in another. Until they divided into neighborhoods, the two sides would argue with each other over the back fences about whether or not to grow carrots in their summer gardens. Violence was actually taking place as noneaters would try to rip out the tender young carrot plants to be sure the young noneater generations did not fall victim to temptation. Separate neighborhoods seemed the only way to save the town.

Even restaurants were carefully marked to let patrons know what sort of establishment they were entering. Some restaurants proudly displayed a three-inch golden "C" on the window by their front door indicating they served carrots on their menu, while other restaurants had a black "C" in a red circle and slash to indicate no carrots were on the menu there.

Several months ago the pastor of the Central Church, the largest, oldest, and most influential church in Quarrelsville, tried organizing a series of forums in an attempt to both clear the air and bring the two sides a little closer together. At the very first forum when recent scientific information suggesting carrots may even have some healthful benefits to those who eat them was introduced, all of the noneaters present angrily jumped up and left, charging biased secular propaganda was being introduced into what was obviously a spiritual matter. At this point the pastor became so disheartened an emergency meeting of the church board was called at which the pastor's letter of resignation was tendered.

The old Central Church had been a part of the Quarrelsville community from the day the town was founded. In fact, the very first property identified in the land register by the founders was the plot where the church was to be built. The first nonresidential building completed in Quarrelsville was the Central Church building. Because of its heritage, neither the eaters nor the noneaters were willing to concede the church to the other side.

When the new pastoral family arrived, they came to a congregation that was seriously divided. In the first worship services the new family attended, the eaters sat on one side of the center aisle while the noneaters sat on the other. All eyes were glued on the pastoral family waiting to see on which side of the aisle they would sit. To everyone's surprise they sat in the balcony.

And then came the "Welcome to Our Church" pot luck held for the pastoral family. No one could have anticipated the events of that evening. Everything went fine until the pastor's nine-year-old unwittingly picked up a luscious looking piece of carrot cake and ate a bite. A terrible scene then occurred at the pot luck between the eaters and the noneaters that precipitated a rancorous church business meeting at which it was announced "The Pot Luck Explosion," as it came to be called, represented the last straw for both sides and how each now felt a split in the church was inevitable and lawyers were retained to accomplish a division of the property.

Of course, as the "once upon a time" should have told you, this was just a silly story. No one creates a division in the church over something as simple as food, do they? In our passage today, Paul is noting the eating or not eating of certain foods was exactly the issue coming between some members of the early church. Another division Paul speaks of was apparently over which day of the week was the proper day for Christians to worship.

Divisions in the local body of Christ more often than not occur over precisely these clearly secondary matters. Do we open or close the church windows? What temperature should the church thermostat be set to? What color will the new carpet be in the sanctuary? Who picked that terrible color paint for the walls in the education building? Will we or won't we have regular pot luck meals? Who is responsible for having a church newsletter, and who gets to decide what goes in it? Should the church worship service start half an hour early and get out in time for everyone to arrive before the lunch rush at the restaurants? And on and on we could go.

More often than not, we find ourselves arguing and fussing over little matters that have absolutely no relevance to the true meaning of the good news. It is rare that matters like Martin Luther's rediscovery of personal faith should divide us. We would rather divide over who will control what group or be the chair of what committee in the church. It is rare that revitalizations of the church like Wesley's or Campbell's movements should divide us. We would rather argue over which is the only acceptable form of holy communion or which is the true and correct translation of the scriptures we should use in the worship service.

Honestly, we have not changed much from the times of the early church. Paul's words to the Romans sound as a ringing fire bell warning us and reminding us of who we really are. We are the servants and not the masters. Who assigned us the task of judging our fellow Christians? We are each to serve in the best way we know how and leave the judging up to Christ. If we are truly about living our lives to serve Christ and others are truly about living theirs to serve Christ, then there will be greater witness and wonder in the glory of God's love for our diversity and the uniqueness we were each created with than would ever be accomplished were we each forced to strive to meet some rigid standard of uniformity set for church members.

The message of the gospel is that God loves each one of us as individually unique and maybe eccentric as we each might be. The second half of the gospel is that Christ is calling us to move our focus away from all of the secondary matters of life and focus on the cross and the resurrection and the price that was paid for every one of us. With God's help in the process, maybe we may finally learn to truly love each other and be the loving witness the church was created to be.

Prayer

O God, you have been so patient with us as we have divided and argued over issues that when viewed in the light of eternity, hardly matter at all. We give you our love today Lord, and we give you permission to teach us how to walk the path of the cross and to love one another. In Christ's holy name we pray. Amen.

Visions and Prophecy

Call

Let us gather in the house of the Lord, all who would hear and proclaim the living gospel of Christ!

Prayer

O God, in your divine wisdom you have chosen in these last days to place the mantle of ministry on the shoulders of all who would be called Christians. Male or female, master or servant, each of us must proclaim the word of the Lord. Give us the strength and the courage to use the gifts you have already given us to boldly proclaim the good news of Christ. In Jesus' holy name we pray. Amen.

Scripture

Acts 2:17-21 or Joel 2:28-32

Hymns

"My Faith Looks Up to Thee"
"O Sons and Daughters, Let Us Sing"

There is probably no more wonderful place to hear consistently challenging preaching than in a seminary homiletics class. Often seminary students, immersed in daily biblical studies and not yet encumbered by what can be some of the more difficult political realities of the pastoral ministry, tend to deliver some very powerful messages straight from the heart. One example of this came as a seminary student a few years ago brought a most dramatic message. The student's sermon was based upon what he very cautiously shared may have been a modern-day vision from the Lord.

In a very conversational tone the student began the sermon by sharing some of the financial concerns that had recently been a burden for his household. Automobile repairs and broken appliances only added to the pressures he felt of meeting the next tuition payment coming due in about a month. Over and over again came the haunting question, "How will all of the bills ever get paid?" Working long hours to earn money and studying for many of the remaining hours each night was actually pretty typical of a seminary student's life.

But then, about a week before this student's turn in class to bring a sermon, came the vision. In the vision the semi-nary student was home visiting his parents for the weekend. It was a beautiful clear winter Sunday afternoon and the sun beaming through the windows generated a warmth in the house that made the crisp January day outside seem far away.

The student's parents were sitting in their living room watching television and snacking on some freshly made popcorn. The buttery aroma of the popcorn filled the house. The student, tired from a hard week at school and not really interested in what was on TV, had gone into a bedroom and stretched out across one of the huge soft beds to take a short nap before driving back to the seminary.

Suddenly the tone of the vision changed and so did the student's voice as he related it. The student was awakened from the nap by some sort of sharp sound that was loud and frightening. He lay there for a moment trying to grasp reality and figure what could have made the sound, when the sound happened again. It was an explosion of some sort and being very sharp and loud it had to be fairly close. But why would there be an explosion and just as frightening to the student, why was everything in the vision now in black and white?

As the student described quickly getting up from the bed and moving to a window in the back of the house where he could see in the direction of the sound, his voice began to quiver. That quiver sent chills through everyone as we realized how even as he was describing the vision for us, he was reliving every emotional moment of it.

The scene the student saw across the field out the back window was terrifying. The explosions appeared to be artillery shells landing. Some unknown enemy was coming, and the artillery shells were coming closer and closer. It didn't make any sense but it would be only moments before the shells would come crashing into their house. He had to quickly leave the house and run. As the student hurried into the living room, his parents were trying to gather up even a few valuables to take along so all would not be lost. Desperately the student cried out, "There's no time! We've got to get out of here and run!"

Together they all ran. Out the door and across the street with nothing but the clothes they were wearing. They ran as hard as they could away from the incoming artillery shells. Running and running, desperately running, they tried to get away. All that was important in the student's mind was that his loved ones somehow get away to safety. Certainly no possessions they had were worth dying for.

Questions screamed through the student's mind as they ran. "What was happening? What was this all about? What was going on?" Finally, in breathless desperation, the fleeing student cried out loudly, "O God!"

Instantly the noise and the violence were gone. Instead there was now a silent calm surrounding the student and out of the calm came God's voice saying, "Exactly! Now you see what is really important in life. God and other people. Nothing else really matters. Remember this as you continue in your ministry." And the vision was over.

Everyone who heard the student deliver that message was held captive by the intensity, power, and the truth it contained. Even those who normally resist-

ed being impressed by other people's sermons knew without a doubt something special had happened in that hour.

In the time since that day many who were privileged to witness this message being delivered have wondered just what it was they saw. From a technical standpoint the sermon was very difficult to describe. It did not have a three-point outline nor did it follow many of the normal conventions usually associated with a good sermon. Yet the message it contained was unmistakably clear and true.

We can hardly have been there and not think of the passage in the second chapter of Acts where the prophet Joel is quoted. The Lord used the prophet Joel to tell us in the last days God would call young men and women to prophesy. To "prophesy" here means to carry God's message to the church—to speak God's word and to restate God's truths for the modern world.

We desperately need God's prophets in the church today. Often the prophetic word is hard for us to hear, and historically, even from the earliest biblical times, we have not treated the prophets well. But if we are to be the church the Lord created us to be, we must be about praying for God to pour forth the Holy Spirit and send us the promised young men and women to prophesy. We must be in prayer for the Holy Spirit to send us the young people with visions and a senior generation with great dreams. And one more thing. We must also pray that God give us the ears to hear and open our hearts to receive God's prophets when they are sent lest we too reject the very messengers of the Lord for which we have prayed as so many generations before have done.

Prayer

Dear Lord, so often we have expected others to carry the ministry of the church while we receive the benefits. Today, Lord, we stand tall and give you permission to pour your Holy Spirit in our midst, giving each of us tasks in your ministry to carry out. Through Christ we lift our prayer. Amen.

No Fear

Call

Let us come together in love to worship, all who would be children of the Almighty God.

Prayer

Dear Lord, through the cross you have called us to become sisters and brothers with Christ. Help us to understand the honor and responsibility involved when we accept the name Christian. In Christ we pray. Amen.

Scripture

Romans 8:31-38

Hymns

"Because He Lives"
"O Love, How Deep"

Shawna had grown up next door to Pastor Earl. When Shawna was very young and she was just learning to talk, she somehow managed to start calling Pastor Earl "Pearl" and through the twenty or so years since, Pearl has always been her pet name for this neighbor and friend with whom she has always been able to share almost anything.

It started when Shawna was finally able to walk well enough to be out playing in their fenced-in backyard. Every year Pearl had a garden of one sort or another along the common fence between their two yards. Little Shawna would stand there visiting with Pearl for as long as he would be out working in the garden. Pearl had almost a magical way of talking with small children, and Shawna soon would get excited just at the sight of Pearl coming out to work in his garden. Somehow Shawna felt Pearl was really coming to see her, and that was how their relationship began.

Over the years, their conversation topics and the locations of their meetings changed. It was not long before the fence was no longer an adequate meeting place for such serious topics of conversation as the latest school yard social events. It did not seem to matter to Shawna that Pearl did not pastor the church she and her mother attended. Pearl's warmth, acceptance, and everyday understanding of life just naturally suggested to Shawna that Pearl knew God pretty well, so he was the one she turned to whenever she wanted to talk about something really serious.

When Shawna was about five, her mother and father divorced. A short time after the divorce, Shawna's father accepted a job which took him to Latin America and except for an occasional letter, Shawna no longer received any contact from him.

Through her junior high years, Shawna was almost a model student. She and her mother had to cut a few corners financially, but with a growing sense of pride, they managed. Sometimes junior high students, however, can be hurtful. Because Shawna did not wear some of the more expensive trendy outfits many of her classmates wore, she began to be the victim of her classmates' barbed and cutting remarks. Not even Pearl could make the pain of rejection go away.

When Shawna turned sixteen, she got a job and began to earn her own spending money. Before long she was dressed as well as anyone and had bought herself a car. It was a major celebration the day she picked up her car. Shawna had saved up for the special occasion, and she had invited her mother, Pearl, and Pearl's wife Edna to be her dinner guests that night and she was going to drive. These were sweet memories.

But now Shawna had asked Pearl to meet her for lunch at a little restaurant half way between her hometown and where she was going to college. Pearl knew something was seriously bothering Shawna, so he agreed to meet her. The whole length of the hour-long drive Pearl asked the Lord to provide whatever wisdom it was going to take to be of some help to Shawna.

When he arrived in the parking lot of the little seafood and chicken restaurant, Pearl spotted Shawna's car already

there. As he got out of the car he thought the simple prayer, "Well, God, let's go see what Shawna wants to talk about."

Once they had ordered lunch, Pearl looked across the little table at Shawna and asked what was happening in her life that she needed to talk about. Shawna prefaced her thoughts with the certainty that Pearl would probably think she was silly, but she could not see how God could love her considering all of the really dumb things she had done in her life.

The warmth and joy that flooded Pearl's soul on hearing these words shone forth in a loving smile and a sparkle in his eyes. Shawna was coming face to face with God's redeeming love in Christ, but how could Pearl communicate this to her? So many times the image of God as our heavenly Father is used, but Shawna had no loving earthly father image to draw upon.

Pearl asked Shawna if she remembered when she was about six and decided to stack up books and chairs to climb up to the kitchen cabinet to get herself some cookies. Shawna remembered. "What happened?" Pearl asked. "You know," Shawna answered, "I knocked the television off the counter and destroyed it." "Then what?" said Pearl. "Mom was furious," answered Shawna. "But did she stop loving you?" Pearl asked taking the incident one step further. "No, I guess not," Shawna replied.

"Or what about the time you forgot to give your mom the message that her brother was in the hospital? Was she angry with you then?" asked Pearl. "Yes, that's the nicest way you could put it," replied Shawna obviously still remembering the explosion around the house that event had precipitated. "Did your mom stop loving you then?" repeated Pearl. "No," came Shawna's answer, "but I think I would have as dumb as that move was."

"And what about the time when you were seventeen and you'd had your job for about a year. You announced you'd had enough of your mom's rules and you were moving out? Did she stop loving you then, Shawna?" asked Pearl with the warmest smile Shawna had ever seen on his face. "No," Shawna replied now, with tears forming in her eyes.

"Shawna, now that you look back on it, can you imagine anything you could have done or that you could do now that would keep you mother from loving you, no matter what?" was Pearl's point making question. Now with tears streaming down her cheeks, Shawna replied softly, "No."

"Shawna, your mom's love is a reflection of the way God loves each one of us. We may be 'dumb' at times, as you put it, and God might not be very happy with our actions, but in Christ, we are still God's children and we are loved. Does that help any at all?" asked Pearl. Smiling broadly Shawna replied, "I understand, and thanks Pearl. I'm hungry! I wonder where our lunch is?"

Prayer

Dear Lord, the idea that you love us so much that in Christ you have adopted us as your children is sometimes so overwhelming we can hardly find it possible to believe. We praise you, Lord, and ask that you forgive us when we complain a little more than we should. Through Christ our Lord we pray. Amen.

Christmas

Call

Come, let us gather together in the house of the Lord, all who would praise God for our salvation.

Prayer

O God, as we hear again the beautiful story of Christmas and the message of your love that it declares, touch our spirits today, that we might share ourselves truly and accurately throughout the world. Through our Lord Jesus Christ we pray. Amen.

Scripture

Luke 2:1-20; Matthew 1:18–2:15

Hymns

"Savior of Nations, Come"
"O Come, O Come, Emmanuel"

The Christmas season is full of many warm and wonderful images and traditions in today's world. We sing of open fireplaces and being home with the family where tables full of food await and gifts will be exchanged. Our Christmas cards often depict beautiful snow scenes with horse-drawn sleighs all decorated with red and green trim and holiday bells. Each year, for a few moments, we pause from the season's rush to sit in warm comfortable pews where we will hear again the story of Christmas sometimes read, sometimes sung, and sometimes reenacted in remarkable ways.

But the story of the first Christmas is not a story of warmth and comfort. There is little of a romantic character in the way Luke and Matthew recorded the birth of Christ. Instead, their images are ones of hardship and rejection for Mary, Joseph, and the baby Jesus.

Think for a moment about when Mary first learns of the Lord's blessing she is about to receive. Mary, betrothed to the fine upstanding man Joseph, hears from the angel of the Lord she will bear a son whom she is to name Jesus. This must have been a time of excitement and joy for Mary, but what must have been her thoughts and feelings when she realized she would have to break this wonderful news to Joseph, her husband-to-be. Matthew shares with us how everything did not go well as Joseph learned Mary was to bear a child. We are not given many details, but we are told Joseph, a man of honor, concludes the only thing for him to do is to end the marriage arrangement with Mary. It is hard to imagine Mary not having felt a bit bewildered and confused at what seemed so clearly to have been God's wonderful plan for her to marry Joseph was now suddenly disappearing like the last rays of sunlight in the evening sky. Again, it is the angel of the Lord who intervenes, and Joseph relents and agrees to follow through with the wedding as planned.

Almost nine months later, not long before Mary's baby was due, a census is announced by Caesar Augustus. Joseph and Mary would now have to travel about seventy miles south to Joseph's ancestral home of Bethlehem to register for the census. In those days, a census often meant increased Roman demands either in the form of more taxes or whatever it was the Romans needed, so this would not be a happy trip.

Going to Bethlehem meant days of long hard travel and Mary, now with the birth of Jesus imminent, was hardly in a condition to travel in comfort. Long days and long nights on the road meant plenty of time to ponder what new taxes the Romans might be wanting as mile after mile of dust and discomfort had to be traveled.

Bethlehem was a crowded place as Mary and Joseph arrived. People filled the streets everywhere arriving to register for the census—people whose lives had been disrupted and imposed upon by the hated Romans. The Jews, already feeling oppressed and overtaxed, were hardly full of a holiday spirit. Tempers were short and the town's facilities were stretched beyond their limits, all for the sake of the Romans and their ever-increasing desire for more and more from the Jews. It was in this stressful and tense atmosphere that Joseph and the expectant Mary would seek a place to stay and be turned away again and again.

But finally, Joseph and Mary would be allowed to seek shelter from the elements in a stable with the animals. It is only reasonable to assume that, with the inns of Bethlehem overflowing, the city's stables would also be full. And it would be here among the sights and sounds and smells of a crowded stable that Christ would be born. Jesus would come into our world not among the scents of pines or cinnamon or the wonderful aromas of holiday cooking, but among the scents of musty straw and sweaty animals in a dirty stable amid an angry overcrowded city begrudgingly responding to the commands of hated foreign rulers. Is there little wonder few in Bethlehem seemed to notice or be concerned about the stars in the night sky or angel choirs?

But it was here, indeed, amid all of this turmoil and bitterness in a stable most would have said was unfit for human habitation, that Jesus was born. Jesus, the Christ, come that all of humanity might know God's mercy and salvation, entered life not surrounded by sparkling lights and tinkling sleigh bells but amid the most humble of surroundings that foretold the ministry the Christ was sent to bring.

But the rejection had only begun. For although few among the Jews seemed to notice or care their Messiah had been born, others were paying close attention. As the magi arrived, reasonably assuming Herod's court would be the place to find the newborn king of the Jews, Herod himself becomes concerned and issues the order to find and kill Jesus. Again, the angel of the Lord intervenes and warns Joseph to take Mary and Jesus and flee to the safety of Egypt until Herod is no longer a threat.

Joseph and Mary, now with the newborn Jesus, must travel. Their trip to Egypt would involve hundreds of miles of dirt, danger, and discomfort. Joseph was a carpenter, not a nomadic shepherd used to constant travel and surviving in the wilderness. But with God's help, they did survive.

And now we have begun to hear the wonderful news of Christmas. Through all of the hardships and rejections, as a witness of God's presence and help, Joseph, Mary, and Jesus survived! Mary and Joseph listened to God's angels and followed God's leadership and step by step through one incredible journey after another, they survived!

Jesus—Emmanuel—literally means "God with us," and this is the message of Christmas. Not the gifts or the candles or the cakes or the candies or even the family dinners, but God is with us. God is with us in the times when we are fleeing to save our life in the middle of the night to Egypt. God is with us in the dusty hard journeys we are led to make for the Lord. God is with us even when we are bedded down in the stables of life, basically unfit for human habitation. God is with us.

The message of Christmas is one of comfort and not one just for the comfortable. So for those whose hearts are broken or weary; for those whose life right now seems desperate or maybe almost impossible; for those whose life is colored with the agony of failure or maybe even the emptiness that comes with worldly success; to you we proclaim the good news. Take heart! Christ has come! God is with us and will walk with us every step of the way forever. People, in the truest sense of God's love, hear the good news, "Merry Christmas!"

Prayer

Dear God, Christmas is such a busy and hectic holiday and sometimes we fail to hear the message you came to share with us. Right now, Lord, we take this moment to thank you for all of the times you did not give up on us. We thank you for all of the love and patience you have shown us. And in the simplest and most heartfelt way, we thank you for the gift of Christmas. We praise you, Lord. In Jesus the Christ's name we pray. Amen.

Easter

Call

Let us gather together this Easter Day and proclaim for all the world to hear, Christ lives!

Prayer

O God, we thank you for the gift of the cross and the resurrection. We thank you for the promise of your grace and your mercy. We thank you for extending to us your healing love. Touch our hearts this morning, Lord, that our faith might be bold and strong as we carry your Love to the world. Through Christ our Lord we pray. Amen.

Scripture

John 20:1-21

Hymns

"He Lives"
"Easter People, Raise Your Voices"

Have you ever done something you wished you hadn't done? Even right at the moment, you knew deep down and through and through you should not have done that.

There is the humorous home safety story about a fellow who is having a bit of plumbing problem. It seems the main drainpipe coming down from the second floor of their house is backing up so he decides to go to a plumbing supply store and buy the strongest commercial drain cleaning liquid he can talk them into selling him. When he arrives home our handyman figures the best place to pour the drain cleaner into the main drain is through the plumbing vent on the roof, so up the ladder he goes. Now some two stories in the air the fellow carefully walks across the wood shake roof to the plumbing vent, opens his drain cleaner and begins to pour it down the vent. Suddenly, to his surprise, a small cloud of wasps that had been building a nest in the vent flies out in protest. Our hero scurries quickly across the roof to safety and he could be heard saying, "Oh, I wish I hadn't done that!"

Now standing at some distance from the vent watching as the drain cleaner takes its toll on the angry wasps, our handyman suddenly begins to notice little columns of smoke beginning to curl up here and there along the path of his hasty retreat and he realizes he has spilled the drain cleaner on the roof. Again he was heard to say, "Oh my, I wish I hadn't done that."

Now he figures the best course of action is to quickly get a water hose up on the roof and wash the drain cleaner off before serious damage is done. He drags a water hose up on the roof and, standing on the very peak, he proudly washes the wood shake roof down and figures he has solved the problem and saved all those plumber's charges as well.

Now anyone who knows anything about a wood shake roof knows aged wood shakes tend to get very slick when they are wet and sure enough the next thing our poor handyman knows he is sliding off the edge of the second floor roof headed for a very rough landing. Shaken but not seriously hurt, he looks up at the roof and says, "I really wish I hadn't done that!" Now as if all of this were not enough, no sooner than he gets his thoughts collected after his fall, but our handyman hears his wife open the second-floor bathroom window and shout down to him, "Honey, you must have gotten the wrong vent. The tub here in the bathroom is still backing up."

Anyone who has ever gotten into a project like that can surely empathize with our hero, but this is not really the sort of "I wish I hadn't done that" we're thinking about today. The type we are looking at today are those times when maybe we gave our word, but then for one reason or another, we did not keep it and we left someone feeling hurt and neglected. Or the times when possibly we said the wrong thing or were misunderstood and someone was hurt by our words. We're looking today at the heart-wrenching agony we feel when we wish we hadn't done or said what we did, and we know there will never be a way to completely undo the damage we've done.

Now you are probably wondering why in the world are we thinking about feelings of guilt and regret and personal failure on Easter morning. And the answer is because these feelings are at the heart of the genuine message of Easter. Think of all the emotions and anxieties that must have surrounded the troubled souls of the disciples that first Easter morning. Only the Thursday evening before they had celebrated the Passover with Jesus. They had been proud of Jesus and what they thought he represented and each had given his word to stand by Jesus whatever would come. The scriptures tell us in detail only of Peter's personal denial, but they all failed and they all ran or denied being followers of Jesus at some point between Thursday night and Sunday morning.

Can you let yourself imagine the grief and confusion and disappointment the disciples must have felt as Jesus was arrested, publicly ridiculed, and finally crucified while they stood helplessly by watching? Can you sense the hopelessness and yes, maybe even the anger and bitterness they experienced toward Jesus, the one they had loved, believed in, and trusted and who it appeared had let them down and abandoned them to the destructive powers of the world? Can you agonize through the nights with the disciples as each must have wondered how they would ever regain some sort of normal life, assuming, of course, they survived at all?

But this is Easter, you protest! Jesus was resurrected, and they hear the good news, the gospel, today. Let's think for a moment, about what hearing Jesus had been resurrected might have meant to the disciples. Would this be good news, without reservations, to the disciples who had failed in their promises to loyally stand by Jesus? Have you ever betrayed or let your best friend down? Have you ever disappointed someone you cared more about maybe than even your own well-being? After you did, what were your feelings the first time you knew you would be coming face to face with that person? Hard, wasn't it? But the resurrection was true! Jesus had been raised from the dead, and John describes for us how Jesus sent Mary Magdalene to carry the wonderful news to the disciples.

And John describes that first meeting, behind closed doors, when Jesus and the disciples again stand face to face. Jesus

137

came to the disciples and his first words were, "Peace be with you." Peace, not meaning the absence of open warfare, but peace meaning an inner harmony—an absence of anxiety and stress. Peace, not referring to some arbitrated truce between enemies, but meaning through God's unilateral decision, there are no ill feelings standing in the way of their relationship. Jesus, always sensitive to our needs, could have chosen no more loving words than these for the disciples. It is Easter, and the resurrection is real.

So where do *we* stand before the Lord today? One of the reasons we can maybe know a little of how the disciples must have felt is because we too have failed and come up short before God's call on our lives, just as did the disciples. We too have had our "I wish I hadn't done that" experiences. We, too, know in our hearts the anxiety one can experience when we've let that most special person down. Where do we stand? We are gathered together, just as were the disciples, and the Lord is in our midst. Hear again then the words of our Lord! "Peace be with you."

Praise God, this is Easter! Praise God, the cross and the resurrection are real! Praise God, we are forgiven! Let us go into the world and with our lives and our voices, praise God!

Prayer

O Lord, again we thank you for loving us so much you were willing to accept the cross. We thank you for loving us so much that, even when we have stumbled, fallen, and betrayed you, if we will only seek your forgiveness, you will give us your peace. Thank you Lord. We love you. In the name of the risen Christ we pray. Amen.

Mother's Day

Call

Let us lift our voices in praise for the loved ones who set our feet upon the pathway of the Lord in the days of our youth.

Prayer

Dear Lord, in your wisdom you shared with us the pains and joys of parenting. You gave us the wonders and the sorrows of both being children and joining you in the creation and caring for our children. We praise you today, O God, for being our most holy parent and we ask that you richly bless our earthly parents.

Scripture

Luke 1:46-47

Hymns

"Lo, How a Rose E'er Blooming"
"I Love to Tell the Story"

This probably seems like a most unusual scripture text for Mother's Day, but in a way it is not really. Surely Mary, like almost every young Jewish woman, dreamed as a youth of not just being a mother, but of being the mother of the Christ, God's chosen one who would restore the kingdom of God among the

Jews. Her heart celebrated now as this new life in her was about to begin.

Mary could only wonder what her child would be like and how these magnificent things were to come to pass. And is it not so very normal for a mother to ponder these questions? Certainly every expectant mother dreams of her unborn child and the great contributions that child will make to the world. Are there not moments when, sitting in the warmth of the spring sunlight, a mother-to-be might smile from within her soul and know something wonderful will surely come through this little life now turning and kicking in her womb?

For there is a special bond between a mother and her child, and although it is a bond that is not really subject to explanation, it begins in these days when the two are one. It is a bond that will be in the loving mother from the day her child is born until the day death separates them in this life. It is a bond that reflects itself in the most intense ways, but it is not always spoken. For who can put into words those feelings when a mother first holds her child and nurses it? Who could put into words the feelings she has when those tiny little fingers touch her and wrap around her finger for the first time? Who could put into words the feeling of a mother as her child sleeps securely in her arms?

Or how can one explain the deep sense of tension a mother feels when she sees her child growing through the stages of life and accomplishing the necessary growth tasks that each level of youth requires? In her soul, a mother knows with each passing day her child is also growing toward independence and with each level her child achieves, she also knows in her heart that her child will never again be her baby or her one year old. Each photograph she takes is not really just a picture; it is an enactment of the words, "This is the day the Lord has made. Let us rejoice and give thanks in it."

And it does not stop here. Can you imagine what it must have been like around their home as Jesus grew from a young boy into a man? Some would say Jesus was the perfect child and never gave Mary a moment of concern. More likely, Jesus grew up with all the tugging and pulling, exploring and adventuring of most children. We know, for example, that when they all went up to the temple when Jesus was twelve, he worried Mary and Joseph when he disappeared and was among the elders learning.

And mothers today share those kinds of anxious moments when the adventures of childhood reach in and touch them. Even the simple things often seem to bring the most complex feelings in the heart of a mother. Watching her child learn to ride a bicycle, a mother's heart can magically be filled with both the shared exhilaration of success and tugging worry that injury awaits her child's first mistakes.

Surely the special bond between a loving mother and her child is real and extends throughout a lifetime. And it is a bond that allows for a special intense transmission of values in life. Mary, whose heart found favor in the eyes of the Lord, most certainly taught Jesus all about her Lord she loved so much. Imagine the stories she shared with her son. Imagine the quiet times. Imagine, maybe more importantly, the ways she shared her faith just by the way she lived her life.

Yes, just by the way Mary lived her life. It is hard to remember sometimes, but our children learn as much or more from how we live and act as they do from what we say to them. Marie, for example, was an active, bright, hardworking young mother of three. She worked right beside her husband in the business they owned and as a result, the children, as some children did in those days, spent a lot of time around the two of them. Both were devout Christians, but seldom was very much spoken about their faith to the children; they just lived it.

With the passing of time came grandchildren and widowhood to Marie. Marie also literally wore out the cover on her family Bible twice as every day, before anyone else in the house was up, she faithfully read the scriptures.

Is it any wonder then that when Marie suffered a stroke in her eighties her witness of faith continued? There in the emergency room of the hospital, when no one knew for sure if the terrible damage had stopped, and fears and doubts were everywhere, Marie overwhelmed everyone by simply announcing a scripture verse had come to her, Isaiah 41:10 (RSV), "Fear not, for I am with you, be not dismayed, for I am your God; I will strengthen you, I will help you, I will uphold you with my victorious right hand."

What a powerful witness to share with your children. What a powerful witness parents, and maybe especially mothers can have about the reality of Christ in the everyday circumstances of life. And it is a message the children hear even more clearly than all the words we say or even the words they might hear from a pulpit. As parents, family, and loved ones, we, and we alone, are blessed with that special opportunity to share the Lord through our lives. We celebrate today our mothers, for theirs is a special blessing from God. And just as surely we join our mothers in celebrating and praying for our children, for they are the parents of tomorrow.

Prayer

Lord, sometimes we have failed to say thanks when you have blessed our lives with the love of our parents. And sometimes we have failed to appreciate and thank our families for the love and support they have given us in our growing years. Forgive us, Lord, and help us recommit our hearts to living and serving you and to loving and caring for our families. Through Christ we pray. Amen.

Thanksgiving

Call

Let us come together before the Lord and give thanks! Let us know in our hearts the ways of Christ that we might give praise to God!

Prayer

O God, as we gather together at this season of Thanksgiving, hear the praise from our hearts and the songs of joy your love has placed in our souls. But most important of all, Lord, touch our hearts with your love that we might truly share thanksgiving with all you bring into our paths. Through Christ we pray. Amen.

Scripture

Matthew 25:31-46

Hymns

"Behold a Broken World"
"Where Cross the Crowded Ways of Life"

It was another day and another time. The nation openly stated its faith in God. In the eyes of most of its citizens, their country was created and established by God as a shining beacon for all the world to see. The national will was dedicated to being right and to doing right for in their eyes they were God's witness before the whole world. *But it was another day and another time.*

The nation's economy had its good times and its bad times. Through the nation's history, it had its prosperous periods and periods when life was very hard indeed. In the good times, the people thanked God for having rewarded them with many blessings. In the hard times, the nation sought to find what had been done wrong and where they had sinned and strayed away from the faith of their fathers.

And the same was true in the world of power politics. The nation had its times of glory and its times without success. Again, the good times reflected God's reward and blessings, and the hard times reflected the results of having nationally drifted from the true faith. *But it was another day and another time.*

And what of the personal lives for those who lived in this nation? Of course there were those who experienced the good times, the times of wealth and good health. The good times came to those who worked hard and deserved the good things as God's reward for being the godly people they were.

And the hard times came—the times of need and ill health—to those who were not deserving of the good things and were not truly godly no matter how their lives appeared to those around them. Bad things "just happened" to those who strayed away from the true faith.

These people were a very self-centered people. It did not bother them to see hard times in the lives of others around them. The sight of others in bad times triggered feelings deep in their soul of gratitude for their own comfort and thanksgiving and that their lives were not like those before them in need. After all it was God's way to use hard times to correct and guide people and even nations. Those who had much were ordained to have very much and those who had little tended to have very little. Was this not what the scriptures taught? *But it was another day and another time.*

What was the community of faith like in this nation? It was very powerful; in fact, in many ways, the community of faith controlled the government. The faithful controlled great wealth and power. The leaders of the faith lived very comfortably, often expecting the very best out of life.

Giving in the faith often received a good deal of public attention. Much recognition and honor belonged to those who gave much. The larger the gifts, the more influence one had. High visibility for one's generosity was very much a part of the faith. *But it was another day and another time.*

There are probably some of you who believe this message up to this point has been a trick or a trap and what we have really been describing is our own day and our own times. Let us hope not, for this has been a description of the day and times in which Jesus walked among us and gave us our scripture passage for the day. Let us hear the words in Matthew 25:31-46 again, but this time hearing them through the surrounding culture we have just been describing.

(Read the text of Matthew 25:31-46 here.)

Was the day really so different and were the times so unlike our own?

Thanksgiving. It is such a wonderful holiday, or should we say "holy day." In this passage Jesus sets before us God's view of love and how we can truly express our "thanks" for all of the blessings we have received through God's mercy and grace. "In so much as you have done it unto the least of these, you have done it unto me."

God ordained our families, and in so much as we set aside a day where we give thanks to God and worship God and celebrate the loved ones with whom God has so wonderfully blessed our lives, we are probably truly in keeping with the will of God.

But, through Christ, it was also ordained that we are all a part of the family of God and we have each been given the responsibility to care for and reach out to those of our family in need whether they be next door or half a globe away. If we fail to hear the words of Christ, we may well hear one day instead, "Depart from me accursed ones," for we saw those in need and we chose our own comfort.

Let us celebrate Thanksgiving this year with all the joy and warmth and love the world could possibly witness. And let us commit our hearts to giving thanks throughout this coming year as, with God's help, we have the eyes to see and the ears to hear where our help can share God's love wherever we go.

Prayer

Lord, we thank you for your mercy and your love. In so many ways we have failed and fallen so short of the people you would have us to be, yet you have loved us still. Truly we are a blessed people, not because we deserve it, but because you are love itself. Help us to celebrate your blessing and to share it with all the world. Through Christ our Lord we pray. Amen.

Thoughts on Prayer

Moderator: We're here today to think and talk about prayer, to share with one another, to learn and to grow. So let me begin by just asking straight out, "What is prayer?"

Person #1: *(Starts out loud and dramatically, with feeling)* Our Father, who art in heaven, hallowed be thy name . . .

Person #2: *(interrupting)* No! No! Prayer is personal. It must be personal. Like this: "Dear God thou art so loving and gracious. Bring peace and harmony to this troubled world."

Person #3: *(interrupts #2)* What are you saying? Real prayer is only done in private. Ask any clergy person; they'll tell you that's true.

Moderator: That's a good idea. Let's ask a clergy person. *(All turn toward person with "clergy" sign.)* Pastor, what is prayer?

Clergy: Maybe we can think of prayer as ways we talk with God, any way we do it.

Person #1: But God hears the prayer that Jesus taught us best.

Person #2: Oh, everyone knows prayer is a special time and has a special language all its own that God gave us.

Person #3: No, the pastor is right. The language isn't important. It's where you pray, like in church or in your own private prayer closet that matters and where God hears us best.

(All on the PANEL freeze as CHILD sitting off to the side speaks.)

Child: Oh God, Mommy's sick. Please help her. What can I do to help her, too? What do you want me to do? *(short pause)* But God, I don't like to do the dishes. Well, if you think that's what I should do, I will. I'll do it for her and for you.

Moderator: I've heard style and form and place are all important. Is that what prayer *is*?

Person #1: Well in Matthew 6:9 when the disciples asked Jesus how to pray . . . well, the Lord's Prayer is what he taught them. Now, would you presume to try to improve on that?

Person #2: True, but as far as that goes, Paul in First Thessalonians tells us to pray without ceasing. Are you going to walk around through life saying nothing but the Lord's Prayer?

Person #3: Now see, that's not logical. That's why in Matthew 6:5-6 we were taught to seek the privacy of the prayer closet and pray there.

Clergy: But you see, we have so many examples in the scriptures of prayer, and each of you has a good point.

(Freeze)

Child: You know, God, I like knowing you're around all the time. When I get up, you greet me. When I go to school, you go along. Even when I sleep I know you are right there taking care of me. And you help me know right from wrong and keep me out of trouble. You're my best friend. Thanks, God.

Moderator: Are we all agreed then that prayer is conversation with God and may have several different forms? Does the person praying count?

Person #1: Well, I'm convinced Christians will always be heard first, especially when we pray the way Jesus taught us to pray.

Person #2: Only Christians? Don't you think the message of the New Testament is that Jesus came to bring everyone the message of God's love, and if we just approach God with the right respect, we'd all be heard?

Person #3: It's *hearts* people! God hears our hearts! That's why it is so important to be private where our hearts can be heard.

Clergy: You know, some people feel God hears us in the clergy in a special way. I don't think I believe that.

(Action freezes again and the child sings either "Jesus, Loves the Little Children" or "Jesus Loves Me".)

Moderator: In Matthew 18:3-4 we read Jesus saying: "Truly I tell you, unless you change and become like little children, you will never enter the kingdom of heaven. Whoever becomes humble like this child is the greatest in the kingdom." Let's stand and join together, singing (*"Jesus, Loves Me" or "Jesus Loves the Little Children"*).